Essential Endocrinology Knowledge for Starting Out

Noah Y. Russell

All rights reserved. Copyright © 2023 Noah Y. Russell

Funny helpful tips:

Every setback is an opportunity in disguise; approach it with curiosity and a growth mindset.

Prioritize debt management; a healthy balance sheet attracts investors and partners.

Essential Endocrinology Knowledge for Starting Out : Master the Fundamentals of Endocrinology and Take Control of Your Health

<u>Life advices:</u>

Incorporate a variety of fruits and vegetables; they provide a wide range of essential vitamins and minerals.

Engage with the world of smart contracts; they automate and verify contractual processes on blockchain platforms.

Introduction

Welcome to this book, your comprehensive companion to the intricate world of the endocrine system. In this concise yet comprehensive guide, we will embark on a journey through the fascinating realm of hormones, feedback loops, and endocrine disorders.

The endocrine system, a complex network of glands and hormones, plays a pivotal role in maintaining the delicate balance of our body's physiology. From understanding the functions of various endocrine glands to unraveling the mysteries of hormone regulation through feedback loops, we will delve into the intricacies of this vital system.

Our exploration will lead us through the realms of normal endocrine physiology, where we will examine the hierarchy of endocrine glands and the hormones they produce. Along the way, we will encounter growth and metabolism endocrine disorders, including growth hormone disorders, pancreatic disorders, and thyroid disorders, shedding light on conditions like hyperthyroidism and hypothyroidism.

The journey doesn't stop there. We will delve into the interplay between the reproductive system and endocrine disorders, exploring topics such as menopause, gynecomastia, hirsutism, and erectile dysfunction, each contributing to a comprehensive understanding of the intricate relationships between hormones and reproductive health.

Beyond the surface of genetics and epigenetics, we will unlock the secrets of endocrine genetics, revealing the impact of our genetic makeup on endocrine function. Epigenetics will also take center stage, unveiling how environmental factors can influence our endocrine system's functioning.

With a focus on the genetics and epigenetics of growth and metabolism, pancreatic function, reproductive endocrinology, and more, we will gain insights into the intricate interplay between our genetic makeup and the endocrine system.

As we journey through the pages of this pocket guide, we invite you to immerse yourself in the captivating world of endocrinology. Whether you are a medical professional, researcher, or simply a curious reader, this guide aims to be your trusted companion in navigating the complex terrain of endocrine health.

Join us as we unlock the mysteries of hormones, delve into the intricacies of feedback loops, and shed light on the multifaceted world of endocrine disorders. May this guide enrich your knowledge, deepen your understanding, and inspire your curiosity in the enthralling field of endocrinology.

Contents

Chapter 1: Introduction to the EndocrineSystem 1
   The endocrine system 1
   Hormones 2
   The endocrine system and feedback loops 6
   Endocrine disorders 7
   Conclusion 8

Chapter 2: Normal Endocrine Physiology 9
   Introduction 9
   Endocrine glands and hormones 9
   Endocrine gland hierarchy 11
   Peripheral endocrine glands 19
   Conclusion 31

Chapter 3: Growth and Metabolism EndocrineDisorders 33
   Introduction 33
   Growth hormone disorders-overview 33
   IGF, GH, and GHR deficiencies 33
   Acromegaly 39
   Pancreatic disorders 41
   DM-overview 42
   Obesity-overview 45
   Thyroid Disorders-overview 49
   Hyperthyroidism 49
   Hypothyroidism 55

- Parathyroid disorders-overview 59
- Hyperparathyroidism 59
- Hypoparathyroidism 63
- Conclusion 67
- Chapter 4: The Reproductive System and Endocrine Disorders 68
  - Introduction 68
  - Menopause and postmenopause-overview 68
  - Gynecomastia-overview 73
  - Hirsutism-overview 80
  - Erectile dysfunction-overview 86
  - Conclusion 89
- Chapter 5: Genetics, Epigenetics and Endocrinology 90
  - Introduction 90
  - Endocrine genetics 90
  - Endocrine epigenetics 91
  - The genetics and epigenetics of growth and metabolism 95
  - The genetics and epigenetics of the parathyroid function 98
  - The genetics and epigenetics of pancreatic function 99
  - The genetics and epigenetics of reproductive endocrinology 103
  - The genetics and epigenetics of postmenopausal status 105
  - The genetics and epigenetics of gynecomastia 106
  - The genetics and epigenetics of erectile dysfunction 106
  - The genetics and epigenetics of hirsutism 107
  - Conclusion 108
- Chapter 6: Links 109

Chapter 1: Introduction to the Endocrine System

The endocrine system

The endocrine system is a network of glands that secrete hormones directly into the bloodstream, controlling physiological events throughout the body (Figure 1.1). Endocrine function and hormone action mediate long-term effects by acting on all cellular processes and systems. They influence growth and development, tissue function, metabolism, reproduction, sexual development, fluid and nutrient homeostasis, and behavior.

Figure 1.1 The major endocrine glands

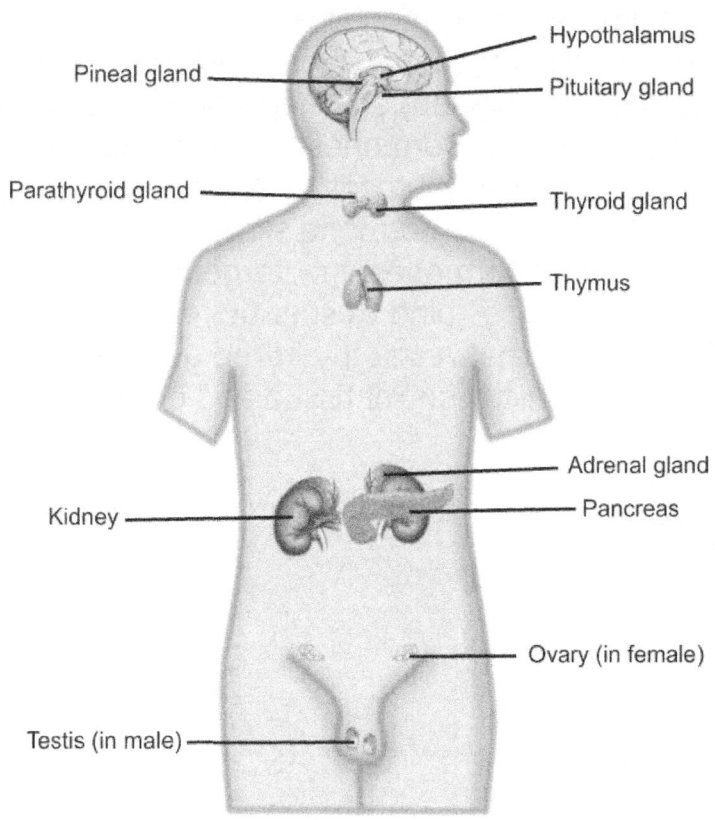

Hormones

Hormones are chemical messengers that relay signals from one set of cells to another via the bloodstream. Most hormone production and secretion is overseen by endocrine glands along the hypothalamic-pituitary axis in the brain. In response to environmental or physiological stimuli, the hypothalamus secretes releasing neurohormones that stimulate the pituitary gland. The pituitary gland synthesizes and secretes hormones that target distal endocrine glands, which in turn synthesize and secrete peripheral hormones.

Endocrine glands secrete hormones via two mechanisms: hormones may be stored in large amounts within cellular secretory granules and released upon stimulation; alternatively, they are continually synthesized and secreted. Hormones target distant cells, bind receptors on the same cell (autocrine hormone signaling), or effect neighboring cells (paracrine hormone signaling). Hormone action is cell-specific, and most hormones only target cells in a particular tissue or organ. Hormones bind to specific receptors and activate intercellular pathways that result in altered gene regulation and protein expression, which control tissue and organ function (Figure 1.2).

Figure 1.2 Hormone secretion and action on target cells

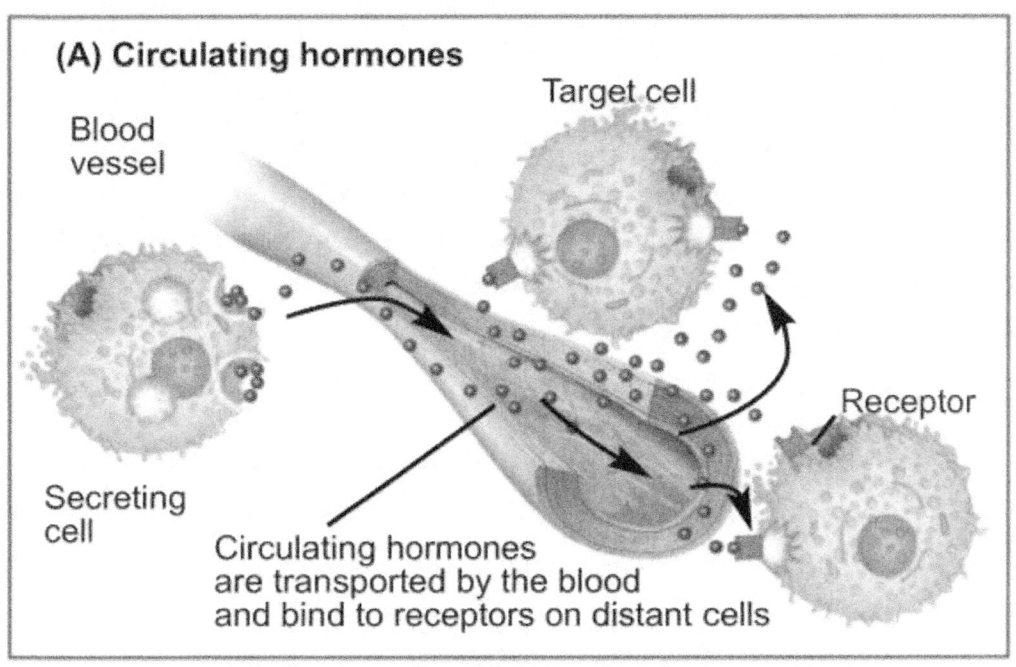
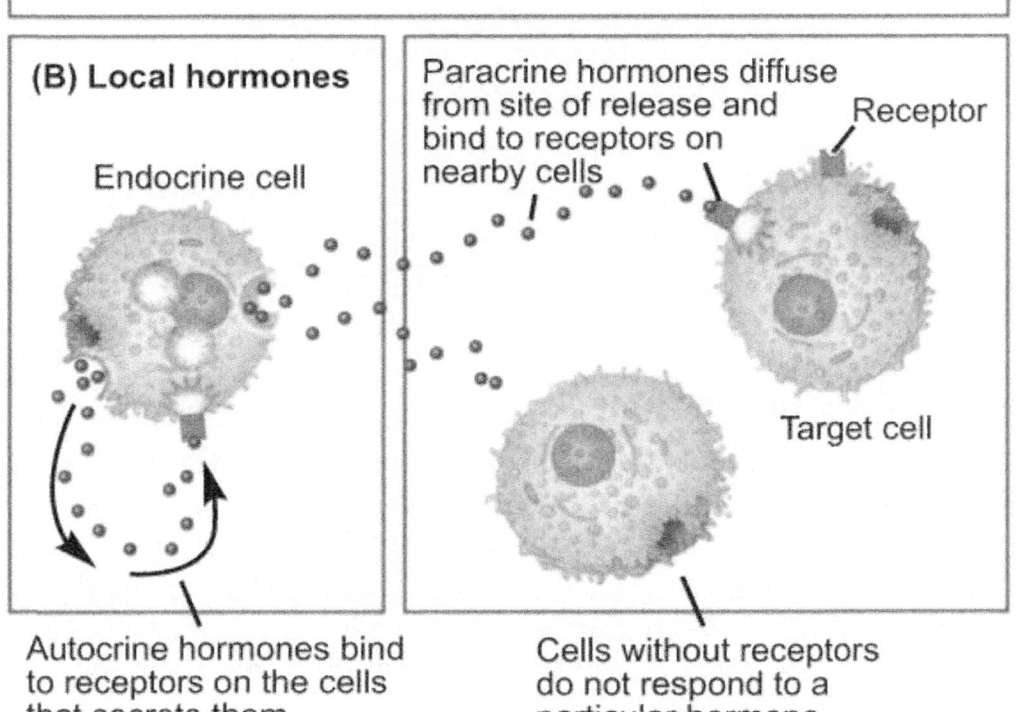

that secrete them	particular hormone

Steroid hormones

Steroid hormones are synthesized from cholesterol and are lipid soluble. They pass through target cell plasma membranes and bind to specific nuclear membrane receptors, forming activated hormone-receptor complexes. These complexes bind DNA and can activate or repress transcription of specific genes (Figure 1.3).

Figure 1.3 Steroid hormone action

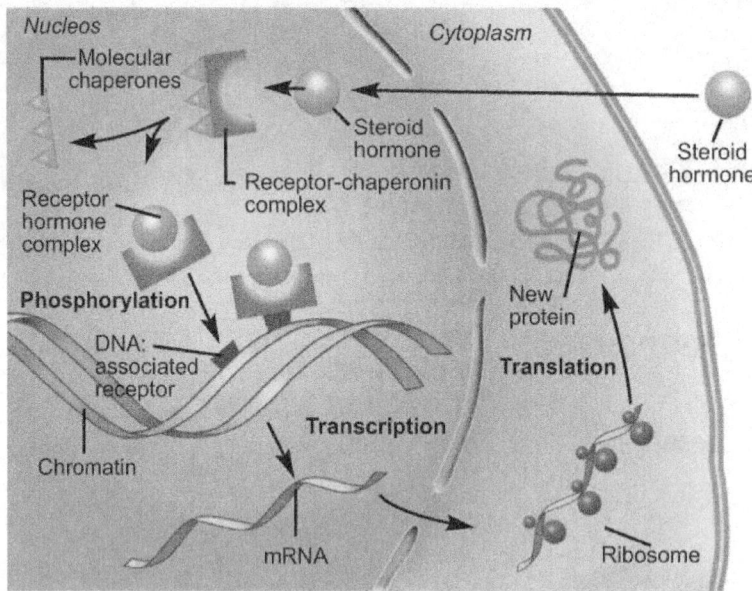

Protein and peptide hormones

Protein and peptide hormones (or nonsteroid hormones) are mRNA translational products that are water soluble. They vary in size; as short as three amino acids, or long precursors that must be proteolytically cleaved to become active. These hormones bind to specific receptors embedded in the target cell plasma membranes. Ligand binding causes a conformational change in the receptor, triggering a secondary messenger cascade (Figure 1.4). There are five known secondary messengers: cyclic adenosine monophosphate (cAMP), cyclic guanosine monophosphate (cGMP), inositol triphosphate (IP3), diacylglycerol (DAG), and calcium ions (Ca2+). All elicit biochemical and transcriptional changes that result in altered protein expression, cellular physiology, and tissue and organ function.

Figure 1.4 Protein and peptide hormone action

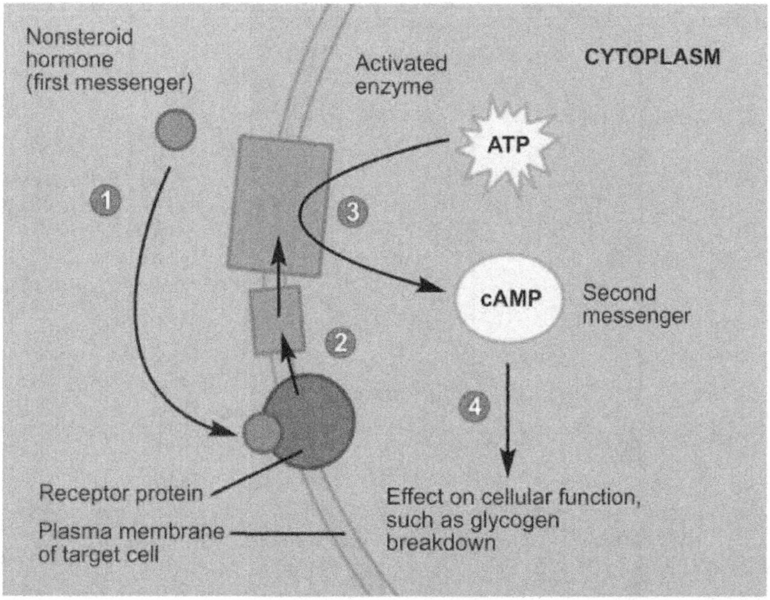

The endocrine system and feedback loops

The endocrine system is tightly controlled by complex feedback loops. Although positive feedback loops do occur within the system, negative feedback loops are more common (Figure 1.5). Negative feedback occurs when the rate of the process decreases as the concentration of the product increases. Positive feedback occurs when the rate of a process increases as the concentration of the product increases. Endocrine feedback loops allow for self-correction and adjustment of hormone synthesis and secretion in response to peripheral stimuli.

Figure 1.5 Endocrine feedback loops

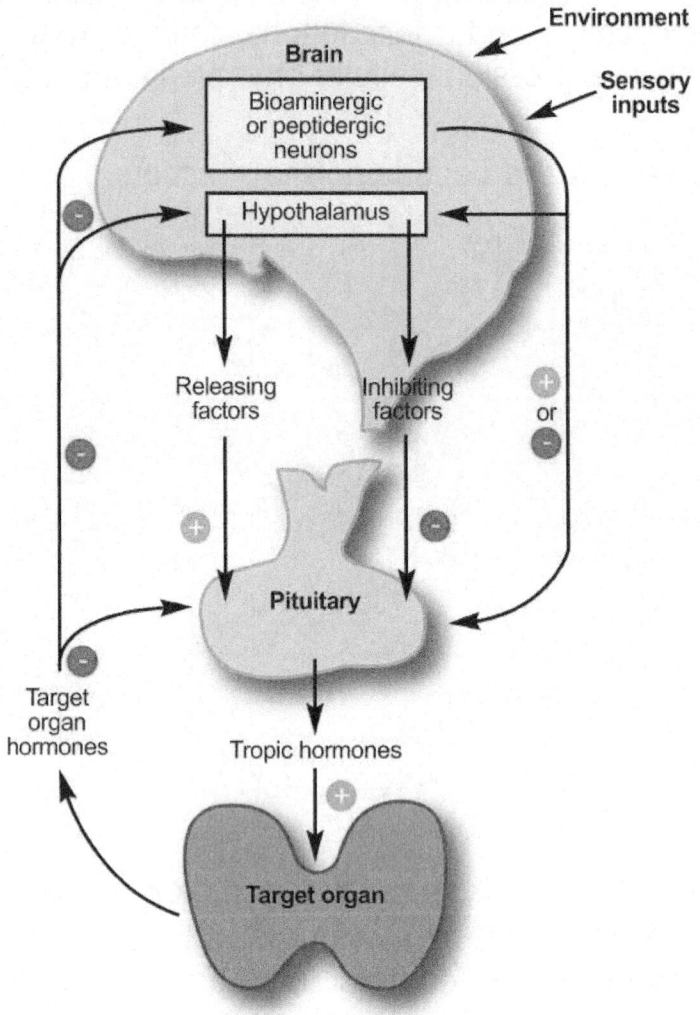

Endocrine disorders

An endocrine disorder is caused by a hormone imbalance. Endocrine disorders result when hormone secretion, synthesis, or actions have failed to elicit a normal target tissue or organ response via specific receptors. Hormone excess is referred to as a hyperactive state. A hormone deficiency is called a hypoactive state.

Endocrine disorder etiology is multi-faceted. It can be genetic, behavioral, or environmental. Endocrine disorders can range from asymptomatic and mild to life-threatening and requiring immediate medical intervention. Etiology, proper evaluation, and prompt diagnoses affect endocrine disorder prognoses.

Conclusion

The endocrine system is a network of glands or organs that secrete hormones targeting specific cells. Hormone synthesis and secretion are controlled by environmental and physiological cues, as well as feedback loops. Endocrine dysfunction results from hormone excess or deficiency. This can lead to disorders or diseases that affect growth, development, metabolism, and the reproductive system.

Chapter 2: Normal Endocrine Physiology

Introduction

Hormones dictate endocrine function. In response to internal and external stimuli, hormones synthesized in endocrine glands are secreted directly into the bloodstream where they circulate to reach their target tissues. Once transported to target tissues, hormones bind to specific receptor proteins that mediate activation or repression of specific genes. Hormone action and response elicits physiological changes that counter stimuli. Crosstalk between endocrine glands, hormones, and hormone receptors facilitate these processes.

Endocrine glands and hormones

Each endocrine gland is responsible for the synthesis and secretion of specific hormones (Table 2.1). Some glands are anatomically and functionally divided according to hormone-synthesizing and secreting cell types.

Table 2.1 Endocrine glands, hormones, and target tissues

Endocrine gland	Hormones (Abbreviation)	Major target tissues or cells
Hypothalamus	Growth hormone-releasing hormone (GHRH)	Pituitary gland
	Growth hormone-inhibiting hormone (GHIH)	Pituitary gland, hypothalamus
	Thyrotropin-releasing hormone (TRH)	Pituitary gland
	Corticotropin-releasing hormone (CRH)	Pituitary gland
	Gonadotropin-releasing hormone (GnRH)	Pituitary gland
	Gonadotropin-inhibitory hormone (GnIH)	Pituitary gland, hypothalamus
Pituitary gland:		
Anterior pituitary	Prolactin (PRL)	Mammary glands, ovaries
	Growth hormone (GH)	Almost all cell types
	Adrenocorticotropic hormone (ACTH)	Adrenal glands
	Thyroid-stimulating hormone (TSH)	Thymus
	Follicle-stimulating hormone (FSH)	Testes, ovaries
	Luteinizing hormone (LH)	Testes, ovaries
Intermediate pituitary	Melanocyte-stimulating hormone (MSH)	Melanocytes
Posterior pituitary	Oxytocin	Mammary glands, uterus
	Antidiuretic hormone (ADH) or vasopressin	Kidneys, circulatory system, CNS
Thymus	Humoral factors	Lymphoid cells, leukocytes
Pineal gland	Melatonin	Hypothalamus
Testes	Testosterone	Many cell types involved in secondary male sex traits including sperm

Ovaries	Estrogen	Eggs, endometrium, CNS
	Progesterone	Eggs, endometrium, CNS
	Inhibin B	Anterior pituitary gland
Thyroid	Triiodothyronine (T3)	Tissues in all systems
	Thyroxine (T4)	
Parathyroid glands	Parathyroid hormone (PTH)	Circulatory and skeletal systems
Adrenal glands: Adrenal cortex	Cortisol and other glucocorticoids	Hypothalamus
	Aldosterone	Kidneys
	Dehydroepiandrosterone	Male sex organs
	Androstenedione	Male sex organs
Adrenal medulla	Epinephrine	Circulatory system
	Norepinephrine	Circulatory system
Pancreas	Insulin (INS)	Circulatory system
	Insulin-like growth factor 2 (IGF-2)	
	Glucagon	Liver

Endocrine gland hierarchy

The endocrine system is controlled by the central nervous system (CNS) and the endocrine glands located in the brain. Upon stimulation, the CNS sends neurotransmitter signals to the hypothalamus. In turn, the hypothalamus stimulates the pituitary gland, whose hormone signaling influences all other endocrine glands (Figure 2.1). The pineal gland, also located in the brain, affects peripheral hormone action.

Figure 2.1 Endocrine system hierarchy

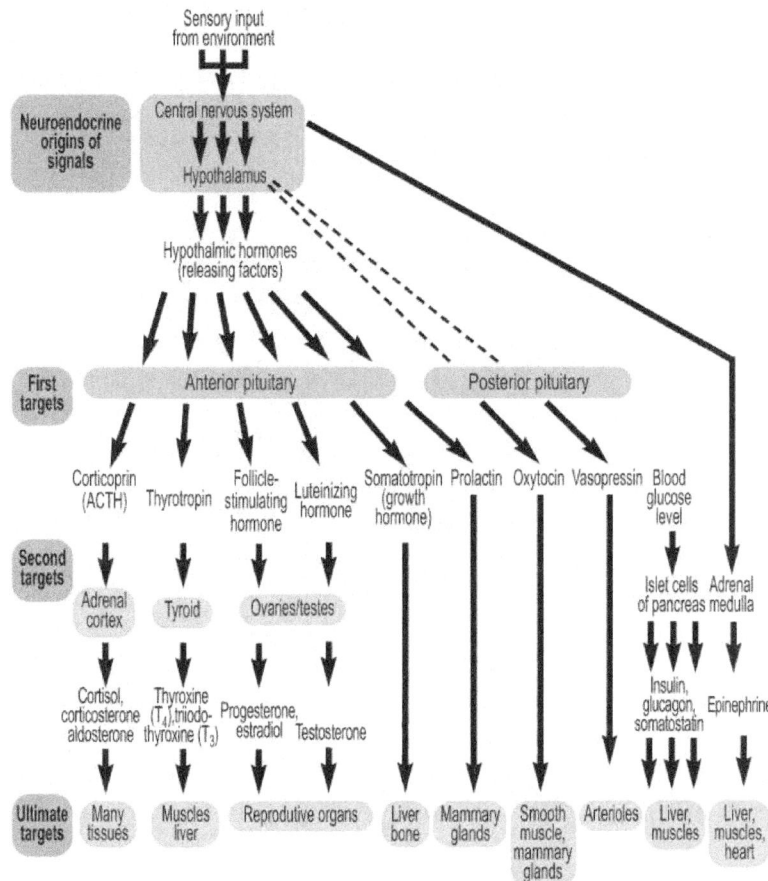

The hypothalamus

The hypothalamus is a small structure in the brain that is anatomically positioned on top of the pituitary gland (Figure 2.2). There is a functional relationship between the hypothalamus and the pituitary that is referred to as the hypothalamic-pituitary axis.

The hypothalamus maintains homeostasis and is multifunctional. It controls hormone release by the pituitary and other endocrine glands, as well as thirst and water balance, hunger, emotions, and sex drive. The hypothalamus connects the CNS to the endocrine system.

Figure 2.2 The endocrine glands in the brain: the hypothalamus, the pituitary gland, and the pineal gland

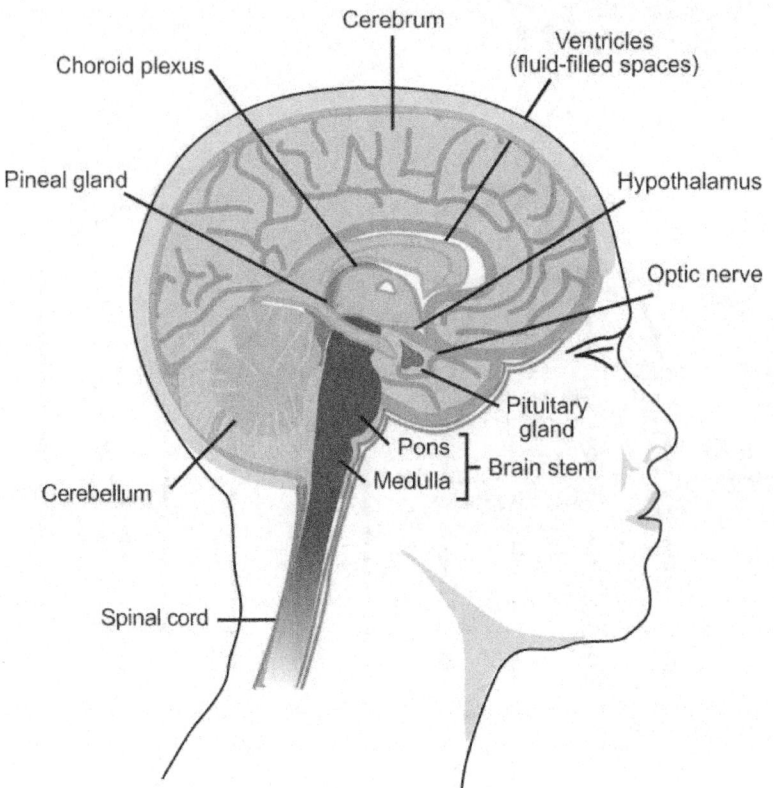

The hypothalamus is composed of neurons that secrete neurotransmitters, neuromodulators, and neurohormones including growth hormone-releasing hormone (GHRH), thyrotropin-releasing hormone (TRH), corticotropin-releasing hormone (CRH), gonadotropin-releasing hormone (GnRH), and gonadotropin-inhibitory hormone (GnIH). These are simple peptides that are released at regular intervals by neural axons into capillaries that carry them to the anterior pituitary (Figure 2.3). Having reached the pituitary, the releasing hormones stimulate the synthesis and release of other hormones that control endocrine gland activity beyond the brain. Hypothalamic releasing hormones and their downstream effects are listed in Table 2.1.

Figure 2.3 The hypothalamic-pituitary axis

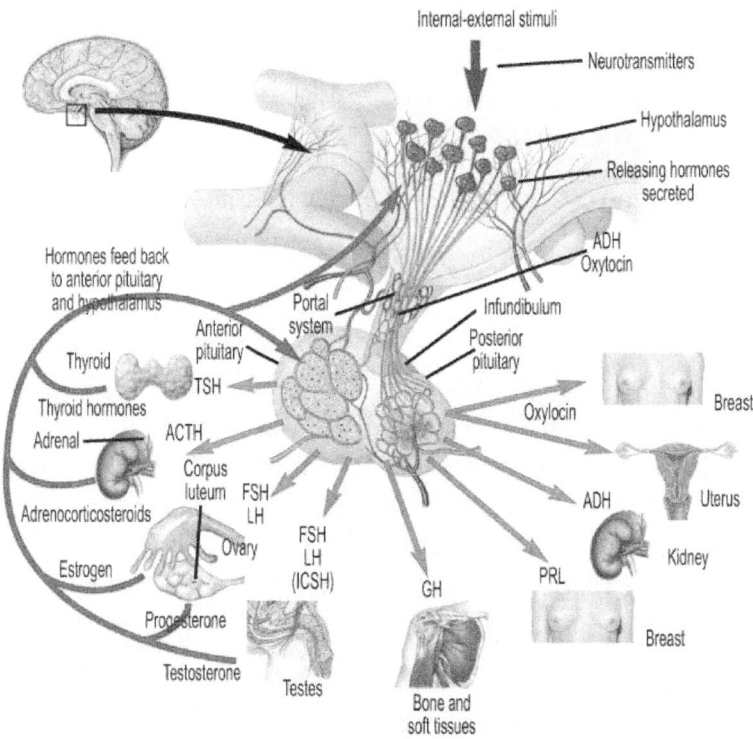

Table 2.2 Hypothalamic releasing hormone effects

Hypothalamic releasing hormone	Downstream effect
GnRH	LH and FSH secretion
GnIH	Inhibits FSH and LH secretion
TRH	TSH and PRL secretion
CRH	Corticotropin secretion
GHRH	GH secretion
GHIH	Inhibits GHRH secretion

CRH: Corticotropin-Releasing Hormone; FSH: Follicle-Stimulating Hormone; GH: Growth Hormone; GHIH: Growth Hormone-Inhibiting Hormone; GHRH: Growth Hormone-Releasing Hormone; GnIH: Gonadotropin-

Inhibitory Hormone; GnRH: Gonadotropin-Releasing Hormone;

LH: Luteinizing Hormone; PRL: Prolactin; TRH: Thyrotropin-Releasing

Hormone; TSH: Thyroid-Stimulating Hormone.

The pituitary gland

The pituitary gland is situated between the optic nerves at the back of the skull (Figure 2.2). It is often referred to as the "master gland" as it secretes hormones that target major organs and other endocrine glands. It acts as an intermediary signaling organ between the hypothalamus and the rest of the body during growth and development, reproduction and lactation, stress, and in response to many other essential physiological processes. The pituitary is anatomically and functionally divided into three components: the posterior, intermediate, and the anterior pituitary gland.

The posterior pituitary (neurohypophysis) consists mainly of projecting neuronal axons. It stores and secretes hypothalamic-synthesized oxytocin and antidiuretic hormone (ADH). Oxytocin synthesis and release from the hypothalamus to the neurohypophysis is triggered by parturition and lactation. Oxytocin is secreted by the pituitary due to vaginocervical contractions associated with birth and in response to suckling during breastfeeding. Oxytocin circulates in the plasma and binds to the oxytocin receptor (OTR) which is expressed in the uterine muscle during late gestation and in breast myoepithelial cells that surround mammary gland alveoli (Hashimoto et al., 2012).

Neurohypophyseal ADH oversees fluid homeostasis by mediating water absorption in the kidney nephron collecting ducts. It also coordinates important physiological processes in the circulatory system and in the CNS. In general, ADH is secreted from the neurohypophysis in response to low plasma levels and increased plasma osmolality. Its secretion contributes to the maintenance of water, glucose, and salt levels in plasma. ADH signaling is dependent upon the vasopressin receptor to which it binds (V1R, V2R, or V3R). Binding to V1R receptors in vascular smooth muscle cells results in a vasoconstrictive action that leads to increased peripheral vascular resistance and arterial pressure; binding to V2R in the kidneys mediates water excretion or absorption; and binding to V3R (or V1b) occurs in the pituitary gland where interaction with corticotropin releasing hormone type 1 receptors contributes to changes in the hypothalamic-pituitary-adrenal axis.

The intermediate pituitary gland is responsible for the synthesis and secretion of melanocyte-stimulating hormone (MSH). MSH stimulates melanocytes in the skin and hair to produce melanin. MSH levels peak during pregnancy and in conjunction with estrogen can increase pigmentation.

The anterior pituitary (adenohypophysis) controls homeostatic maintenance of all body systems. The adenohypophysis's synthesis and release of several hormones is cell-specific. Somatotroph cells produce growth hormone (GH), lactotrophs produce prolactin (PRL), corticotrophs produce adrenocorticotropin (ACTH), thyrotrophs produce thyroid-stimulating hormone (TSH) and gonadotrophs produce luteinizing hormone (LH) and Follicle-stimulating hormone (FSH). Anterior pituitary hormones fluctuate quickly and dramatically in response to central or peripheral physiological stimuli or inhibiting signals from the hypothalamus, the rest of the body, or the environment.

Pituitary hormones and functions are listed in Table 2.3.

Table 2.3 Pituitary hormones and functions

Pituitary lobe	Pituitary hormone	Function
Anterior	ACTH	Adrenal cortex stimulation (glucocorticoid secretion), melanocyte pigmentation
	FSH	Ovarian follicle growth, estrogen production (women); sperm production (men)
	GH	Somatic growth
	LH	Sex steroid production, gametogenesis
	PRL	Lactation
	TSH	Thyroid hormone production (T3 and T4)
Intermediary	MSH	Melanin production
Posterior	Oxytocin	Labor, parturition, lactation,
	ADH	Fluid homeostasis

ACTH: Adrenocorticotropic Hormone; ADH: Antidiuretic Hormone;

FSH: Follicle-Stimulating hormone; GH: Growth Hormone; LH: Luteinizing Hormone; MSH: Melanocyte-Stimulating Hormone; PRL: Prolactin;

TSH: Thyroid-Stimulating Hormone.

Autocrine and paracrine hormone signaling via other pituitary peptides, cytokines, growth factors, and non-pituitary derived hormones contribute to changes in pituitary gland hormone levels (Perez-Castro et al., 2012). All are components of endocrine gland axes and feedback loops that ultimately control pituitary hormone secretion.

The pineal gland

The pineal gland (epiphysis) is also situated in the brain and is considered part of the epithalamus (Figure 2.2). The gland is composed of pinealocytes and is sensitive to circadian rhythms. It secretes the hormone melatonin, predominantly at night, yet melatonin synthesis and secretion are dependent on light exposure in the eye. Light signals are sent from the eye to the superchiasmatic nuclei and pineal gland in order to modulate sleep-wake patterns. Melatonin binds to two G-protein coupled receptors (MT1, MT2) expressed in the CNS (superchiasmatic nuclei, pineal gland, pituitary gland) and many other organs and tissue types throughout the body, including the gastrointestistinal tract, gallbladder, parotid gland, pancreas, breast tissue, major blood vessels and peripheral vasculature, placenta, fetal kidneys, adipose tissues, and specific blood cell types involved in the immune system (Figure 2.4). In addition, melatonin causes the secretion of other hormones by influencing the circadian multioscillator system, has anti-oxidant properties, and affects mitochondrial function (Hardeland, 2012). Melatonin synthesis and secretion is suppressed by nocturnal illumination, and secretion decreases with age (Hardeland, 2012).

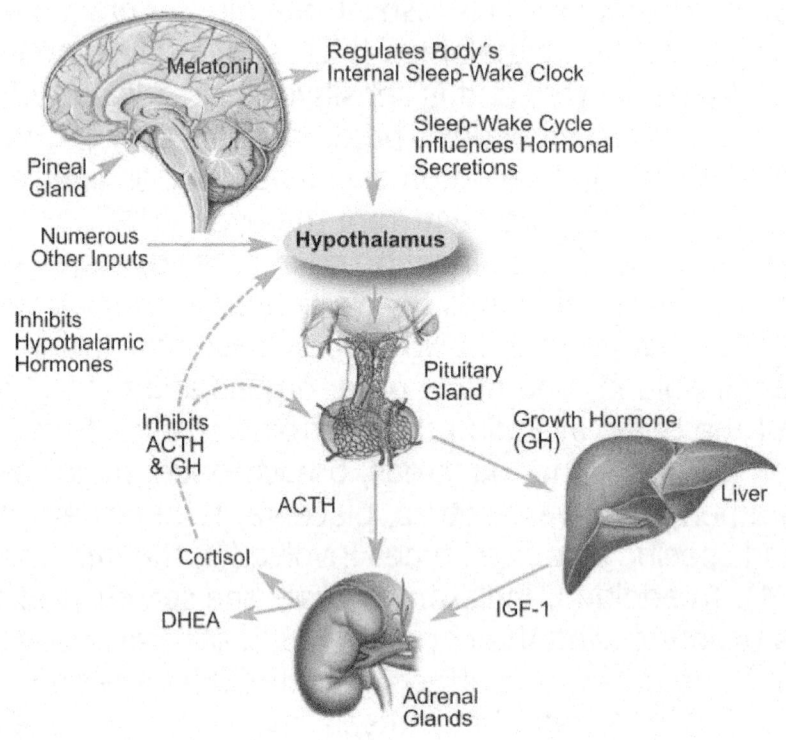

Peripheral endocrine glands

The thymus

The thymus consists of two lobes located in front of the heart but behind the sternum. Its primary function is the release of humoral factors that define lymphocyte and T cell lymphocyte development, differentiation, and function within the adaptive immune system. Specifically, the thymus develops a vast repertoire of T-cell receptors that will be self-tolerant and recognize foreign antigens. Sex hormones, adrenal and thyroid hormones, pituitary hormones, and metabolic hormones all influence immune activation and thymic function (Figure 2.5). The thymus is most active in neonates and adolescents. In adults, it becomes small, and thymus stroma cells are replaced with adipose tissue (Geenen, 2012).

Figure 2.5 Factors influencing thymus function

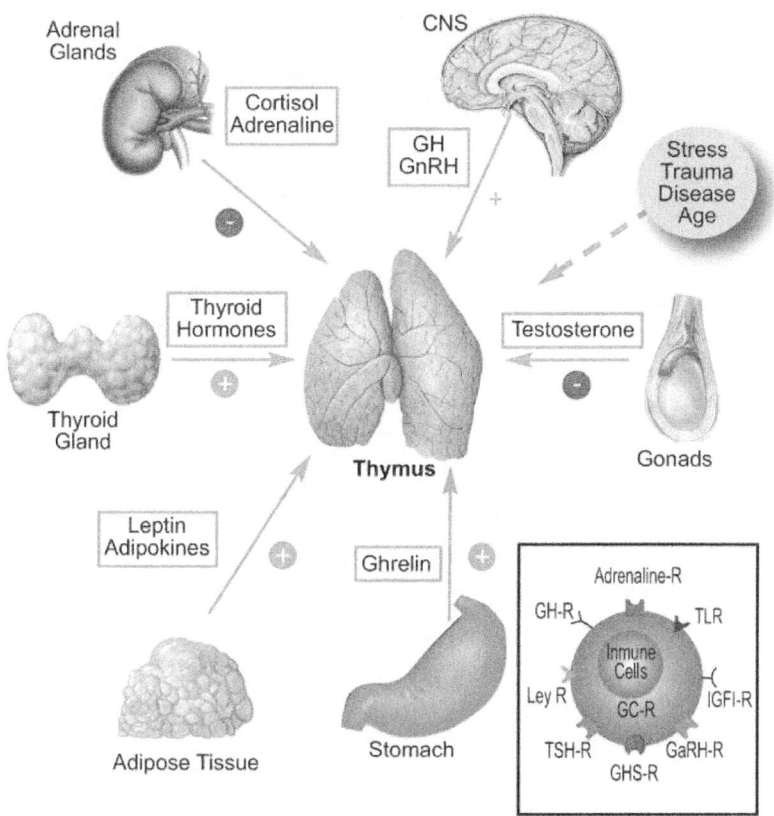

The thyroid gland

The thyroid gland consists of two lobes that lie against the larynx and the trachea in the neck. Thyroid hormones include triiodothyronine (T3) and thyroxine (T4). Synthesis and secretion of both are executed by the hypothalamic-pituitary-thyroid axis (Figure 2.6). Upon stimulation, the hypothalamus synthesizes and secretes TRH, which in turn stimulates synthesis and secretion of TSH by the pituitary gland. TSH prompts the thyroid to release T3 and T4, increasing basal metabolic rate. Elevated levels of both result in a negative feedback loop to the hypothalamus (Schmaltz, 2012).

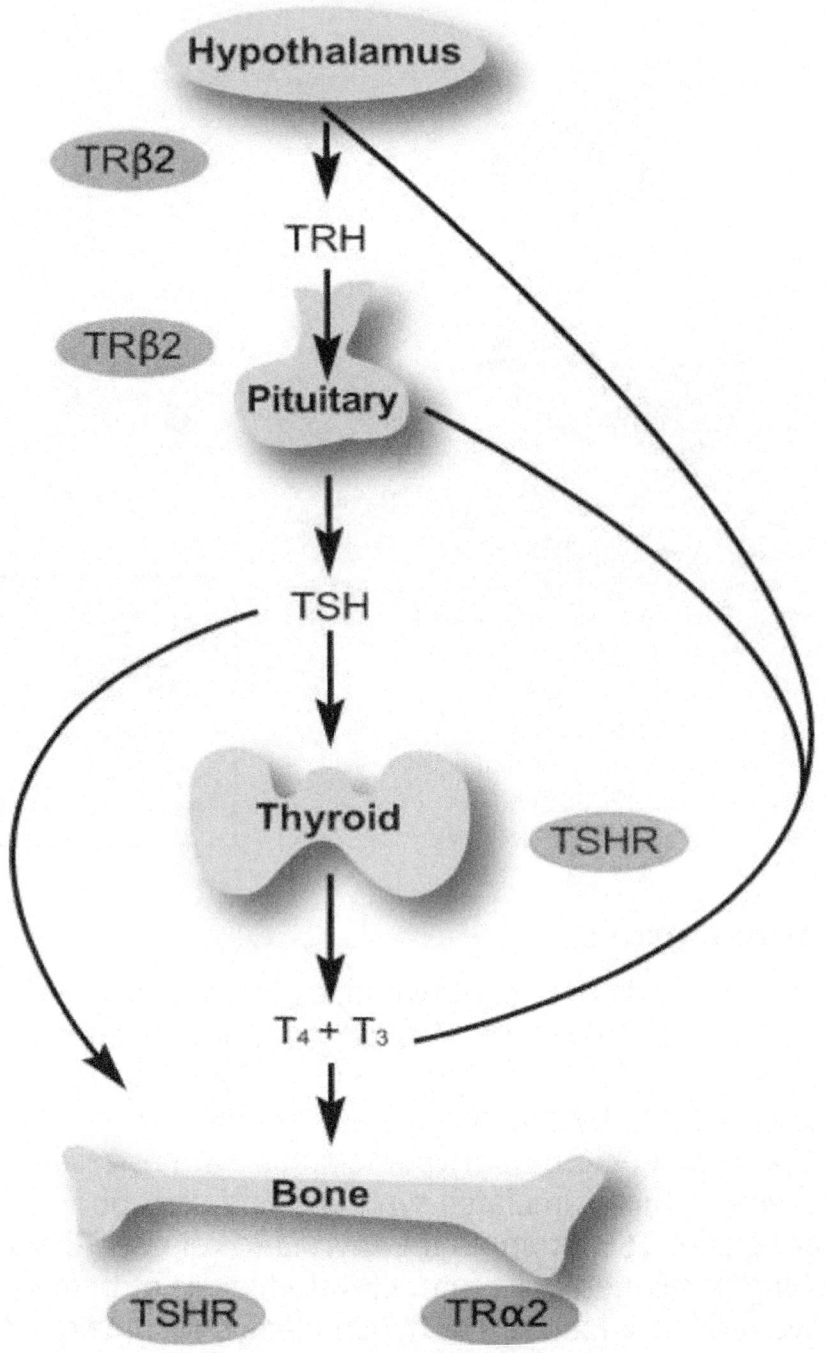

Thyroid epithelial follicles secrete thyroglobulin, a glycoprotein essential for T3 and T4 synthesis. When the thyroid is stimulated by TSH, T3 and T4 are released into the bloodstream where they are picked up by specific binding proteins. They are imported into all cell types in the body, where they bind thyroid hormone receptors (TR) in the nucleus. Ligand binding results in transcriptional activation of mitochondrial genes that increase cellular energy production and of genes involved in cell cycle control and cellular differentiation. Overall, thyroid hormone production triggers many metabolic mechanisms. These include increased cellular metabolism and effective carbohydrate use, increased respiratory rate and oxygen consumption, increased synthesis and secretion of digestive enzymes in the gastrointestinal tract, increased muscle development and strength, regulation of sleep-wake cycles and normal thought processing, increased release of other hormones, and increased tissues' needs for hormones to keep up with an increased metabolism (Schmaltz, 2012).

The parathyroid glands

Four parathyroid glands are located on the back surface of the thyroid gland. The glands positioned higher and closer to the head are called the superior parathyroid glands; the lower glands are referred to as the anterior parathyroid glands. Parathyroid gland function is mediated by parathyroid hormone (PTH) and Vitamin D. All four are responsible for regulating calcium and phosphate levels in the cardiovascular and skeletal systems (Figure 2.7). Coordination of their function contributes to neurotransmitter secretion, nerve conduction, muscle contraction, and activation/deactivation of countless enzymes (Bienaimé et al., 2011).

Figure 2.7 Parathyroid function and calcium metabolism

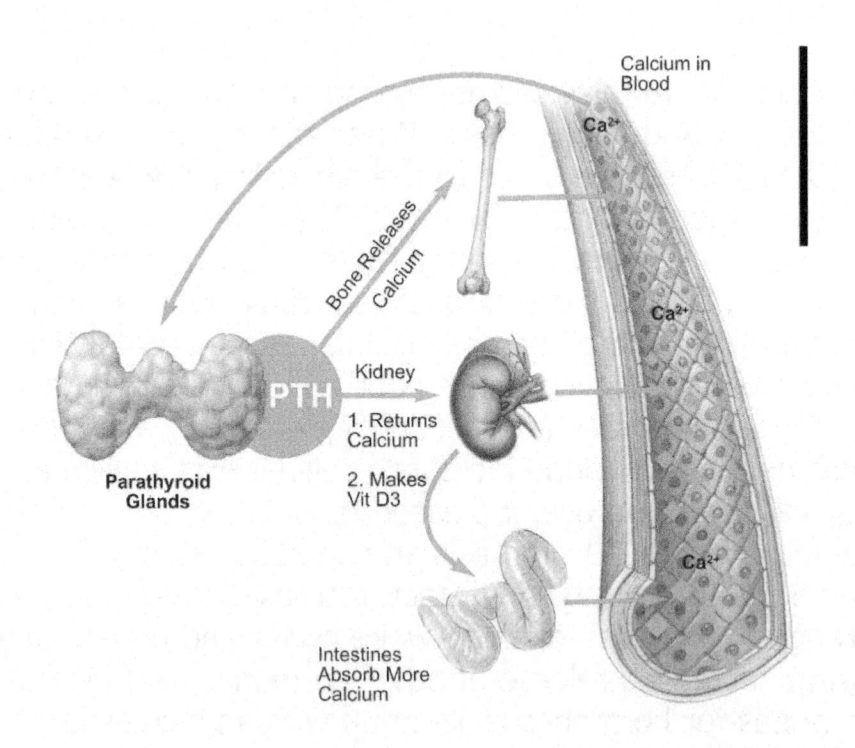

PTH synthesis and secretion is stimulated by decreased Ca2+ serum levels and activation of the calcium-sensing receptor CaSR. Secreted PTH binds to the G-protein coupled receptor PTH-R1 on target cells. In bone tissue, PTH stimulates calcium release via osteoclast cell bone resorption and differentiation. In the kidney, PTH promotes calcium retention via reabsorption in the ascending limbs and distal tubules of the nephron. At the same time, it inhibits phosphate reabsorption in the proximal tubule.

Circulating vitamin D enters parathyroid cells via diffusion and must undergo hydroxylation before it can bind to the vitamin D receptor (VDR). PTH facilitates this process in the kidney. Binding of hydroxylated vitamin D to its receptor activates the transcription of several genes, including CaSR and VDR, and inhibits the transcription of the PTH gene. Overall, this leads to higher calcium sensitivity, higher gut absorption of calcium and phosphate, and calcium resorption in bone cells (Bienaimé et al., 2011).

The adrenal glands

The adrenal glands are anatomically situated on top of the kidneys in the retroperitoneum and differ slightly in shape. The adrenal glands are divided structurally and functionally into the adrenal cortex and medulla. Cells (zona glomerulosa; zona fasciculata) in the outermost layer of the adrenal cortex secrete aldosterone and glucocorticoids such as cortisol. Chromaffin cells in the innermost layer of the adrenal cortex (zona reticularis) secrete androgens. The adrenal medulla synthesizes the catecholamines epinephrine and norepinephrine. Adrenal gland hormone signaling forms part of the hypothalamic-pituitary-adrenal axis (Figure 2.8).

Figure 2.8 The hypothalamic-pituitary-adrenal axis

Stress
Physical, psychological or environmental

- Hypothalamus
- CRH
- Pituitary Gland
- ACTH
- Adrenal Gland (located above kidneys)
- Cortisol

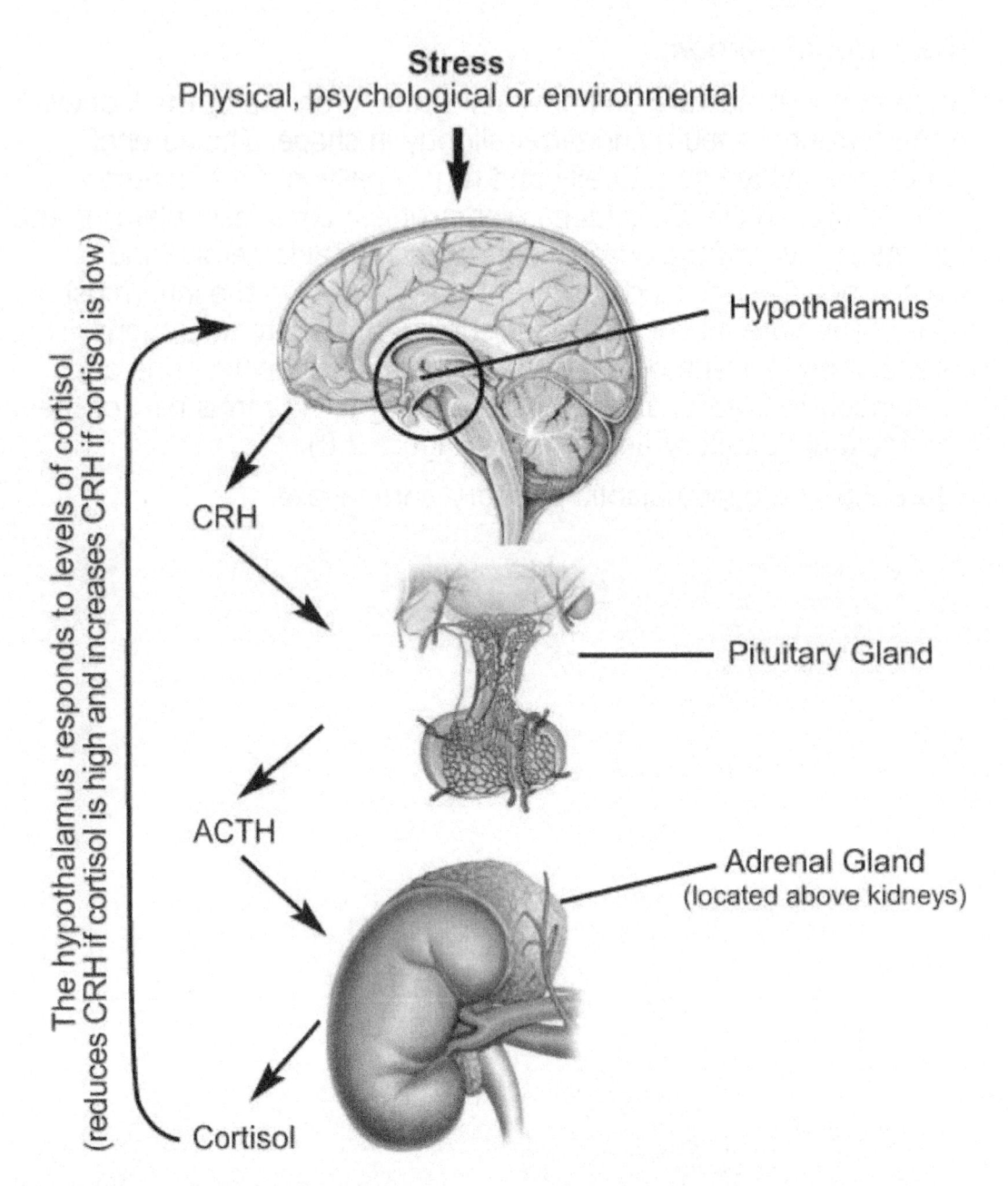

The hypothalamus responds to levels of cortisol (reduces CRH if cortisol is high and increases CRH if cortisol is low)

CRH: Corticotropin-releasing hormone; ACTH: Adrenocorticotropic hormone.

Renal function and fluid homeostasis are highly dependent on the adrenal glands. Aldosterone synthesis and secretion is regulated by several factors: circulating angiotensin II and K+ levels in plasma, and ACTH and endothelin-1 in kidney endothelial cells. First, hypothalamic CRH secretion stimulates synthesis and secretion of ACTH from the pituitary gland. In turn, ACTH stimulates the synthesis and release of aldosterone. Aldosterone mediates its effects by binding to the mineralocorticoid receptor (MR) expressed in the kidneys, colon, brain, and tissues in the cardiovascular system. Upon binding with its ligand, the MR dimerizes and translocates to the nucleus where it mediates transcription of genes that control water and electrolyte balance in the nephron, ultimately contributing to blood pressure homeostasis (Fourkiotis et al., 2012).

Cortisol (or hydrocortisone) is synthesized and secreted in response to stress and low levels of serum glucocorticoids. As with aldosterone, its action is dependent on the hypothalamic-pituitary-adrenal axis. Cortisol binds to the glucocorticoid receptor that is expressed on most cell types. Binding initiates the receptor's translocation to the nucleus where it mediates transcription of genes involved in several physiological processes. They include stimulation of liver gluconeogenesis and amino acid transport from extrahepatic tissues in order to support gluconeogenesis, inhibition of glucose uptake from adipose and muscle tissue, fat breakdown in adipose tissue, and the initiation of a negative feedback loop back to the brain. In addition, cortisol is involved in anti-inflammatory and stress responses. It inhibits infection-induced inflammation by acting on T4 lymphocytes and other pro-inflammatory pathways that involve MAPK, NF-Kβ, and AP-1 (Silverman and Sternberg, 2012). Lastly, maternal cortisol is important in fetal development.

The adrenal medulla secretes epinephrine and norepinephrine directly into the bloodstream and is stimulated by physical or emotional stress. Epinephrine and norepinephrine act as neuromodulators in the CNS and as hormones in the cardiovascular system, preparing the body for the "fight-or-flight" response. Both mediate responses by acting on blood pressure and heart rate as well as serum glucose levels. Norepinephrine also inhibits insulin (INS) secretion from pancreatic β cells (Currie et al., 2012).

The pancreas

The pancreas is a long, tapered gland that lies along the back of the abdomen, behind the stomach. It is part of both the digestive and endocrine systems. As an exocrine digestive gland, pancreatic acinar cells produce and secrete pancreatic fluid into the small intestine (via the pancreatic duct) to aid digestion. As an endocrine gland, β cells in the pancreatic islets (or islets of Langerhans) produce and secrete INS and pancreatic islet α cells synthesize and secrete glucagon.

INS secretion is mainly stimulated by high serum glucose levels, but evidence suggests it is also regulated by other nutrients, circulating hormones, the autonomic nervous system, and paracrine or autocrine signaling (Braun et al., 2012). INS binding to the insulin receptor (IR) in target tissues (the pancreas, liver adipose tissue, CNS) causes structural changes in the receptor that activate its tyrosine kinase function and signaling. Signaling initiates the cellular processes needed for glucose homeostasis (Seino, 2012).

Glucagon is secreted in response to low glucose serum levels, nutrients, neurotransmitters, and INS signaling via other α cells, β cells, and δ cells in the pancreatic islets. Glucagon binds to a G-protein coupled receptor encoded by the GCGR gene. The GCGR protein is mainly expressed in the liver and the kidneys, but is also found in other pancreatic cells, adipose tissue, the heart, spleen, thymus, adrenal glands, CNS, and the gastrointestinal tract. Ligand binding and receptor activation triggers cAMP signaling that leads to increased glucose production by the liver (Cryer, 2012). The roles of

INS and glucagon in glucose metabolism are summarized in Figure 2.9.

Figure 2.9 Pancreas endocrine function

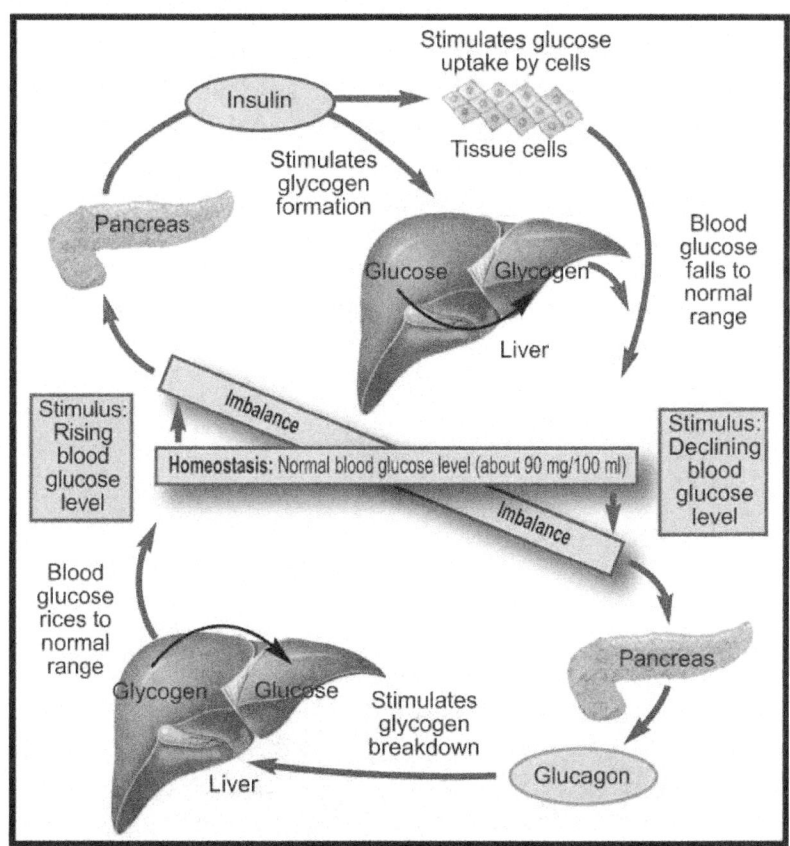

β cells also secrete insulin-like growth factor 2 (IGF-2) which binds to the IGF-1R, IGF-2R, and IR receptors. Although IGF-2 is usually secreted during pregnancy to promote growth, it appears to promote β cell proliferation and regeneration in the adult pancreas (Zhou et al., 2012).

The ovaries

The ovaries are anatomically located in the lateral walls of the female pelvis. They have endocrine and gonadal functions, release estrogen and progesterone, and are the site of oogenesis. Estrogen maintains the female reproduction system and controls the onset of puberty and menopause, Synthesis of ovarian hormones falls under the hypothalamo-pituitary-gonadal axis, which includes a feedback loop back to the hypothalamus (Figure 2.10). Estrogen synthesis is modulated by the secretion of GnRH by the hypothalamus and pituitary release of the gonadotropins LH and FSH. These two hormones stimulate ovarian follicles to synthesize and produce estrogens (17β-estradiol, estriol, and estrone) and progesterone (Christensen et al., 2012).

Figure 2.10 Ovary-synthesized hormones and the hypothalamic-pituitary-gonadal axis.

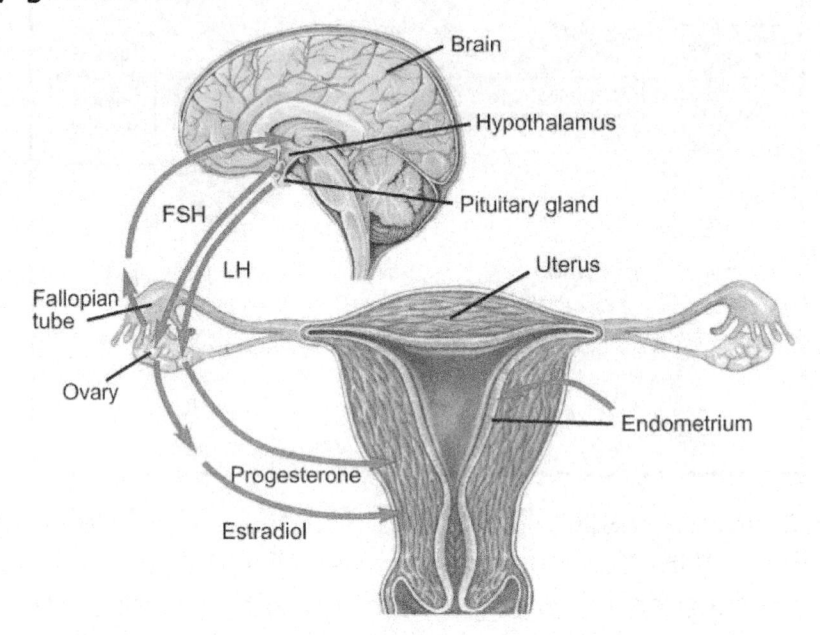

FSH: Follicle-Stimulating Hormone; **LH:** Luteinizing Hormone.

17β-estradiol (E2) is the active form of estrogen that is produced in the ovarian granulose cells and is multifunctional. It creates a negative feedback loop inhibiting GnRH and FSH release, induces ovulation, is responsible for multiple female secondary sex traits, and induces expression of the progestin receptor in many tissue types. 17β-estradiol acts on the estrogen receptors ERα, ERβ, and the estrogen G-protein coupled receptor (GPER-1), and initiates many signaling pathways. Ligand binding may trigger translocation of the receptors to the nucleus to activate or suppress transcription of target genes. Alternatively, E2 binding to its receptors triggers the release of several cellular signaling molecules including calcium, nitric oxide or kinases (Berga and Naftolin, 2012).

Progesterone prepares the uterus for pregnancy and the mammary glands for lactation. Along with estrogen, it is responsible for the cyclic changes that occur in the endometrium during menstruation. In addition, many studies report that progesterone mediates aggression, maternal behavior, learning and memory, mood, and sexual differentiation (Mani and Oyola, 2012). Progesterone binds to its receptor (PR), which translocates to the nucleus to mediate transcription of genes involved in the neural network and female reproductive behavior. Binding of progesterone to PR also triggers signaling cascades that involve calcium, nitric oxide, or kinases (Mani and Oyola, 2012).

The testes

Human testes are normally located outside the body and suspended in the scrotum. The testes are both endocrine and gonadal as they secrete androgen hormones (testosterone, dihydrotestosterone, androstenedione) and are the sites of spermatogenesis. As with the ovaries, testosterone synthesis and secretion is part of the hypothalamic-pituitary-gonadal axis, and under control of hypothalamic GnRH, which stimulates pituitary secretion of the gonadotropins LH and FSH. Testosterone is produced and secreted by Leydig cells in the testes. Both LH and high levels of intratesticular testosterone are needed for normal spermatogenesis. Intratesticular testosterone mediates its effects in the testes by binding to the androgen receptor (AR) expressed on Leydig, Sertoli, and peritubular cells. AR activation results in translocation to the nucleus where it activates transcription of genes (such as IGF1) that are involved in the development and maintenance of secondary male characteristics. In turn, testosterone creates a negative feedback loop directly to the hypothalamus and the pituitary (Figure 2.11). Testosterone also instigates an indirect inhibitory route to the pituitary via Sertoli cell expression of inhibin B (Page, 2012).

Figure 2.11 Testes-synthesized testosterone and the hypothalamic-pituitary-gonadal axis

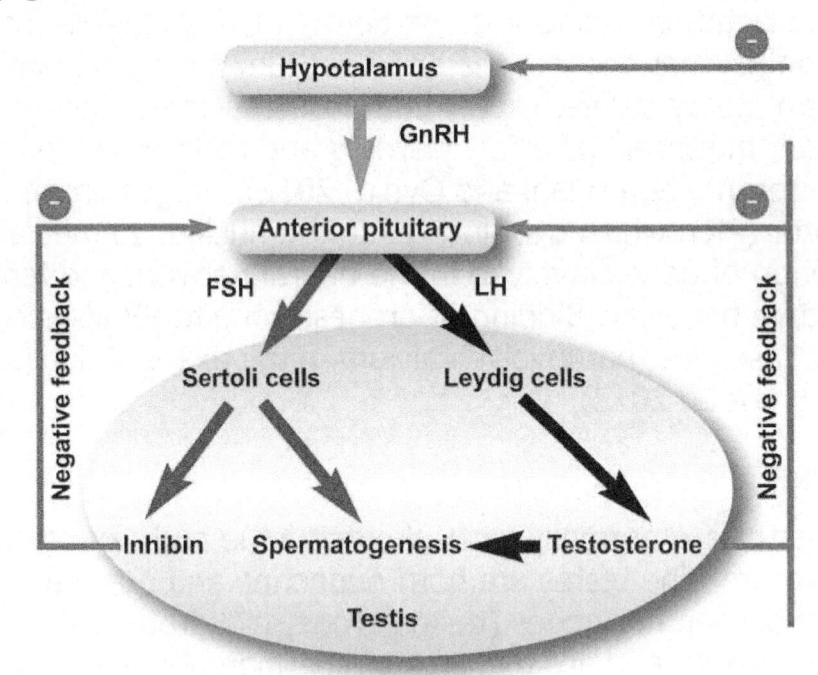

FSH: Follicle-Stimulating Hormone; **GnRH:** Gonadotropin-Releasing Hormone; **LH:** Luteinizing Hormone.

Conclusion

The endocrine system consists of hormone-secreting glands that work together in response to internal and environmental stimuli. Under normal conditions, stimulated hormones act on target tissues or specific cell types, ultimately causing differential gene expression that evoke physiological changes. Hormonal action depends on functioning hormones, secretion mechanisms, and intact hormone receptors.

Chapter 3: Growth and Metabolism Endocrine Disorders

Introduction

Endocrine disorders occur when hormone action or response is compromised, often via hormone excess or deficiency. Both conditions can pathologically alter growth, development, and metabolism. Growth disorders impair the GH/IGF-1 axis, affecting height and development. Pancreatic disorders affect weight, appetite, and glucose metabolism. Thyroid disorders affect overall metabolism and the physical and chemical processes that require energy. Parathyroid disorders affect calcium and phosphate metabolism.

Growth hormone disorders-overview

Growth hormone disorders (GHD) occur when the endocrine factors contributing to skeletal growth are dysfunctional. These include the hormones GH, GHIH (or somatostatin), and IGF-1, as well as their corresponding receptors. GH controls IGF-1, the primary modulator of somatic growth. GH, IGF-1, and GHR deficiencies, as well as elevated IGF-1 levels, can all impair the GH/IGF axis.

IGF, GH, and GHR deficiencies

Primary IGF deficiencies are characterized by normal or increased levels of GH, and insufficient plasma IGF-1 levels are caused by defective GHRs. Secondary IGF deficiencies result from hypothalamic or pituitary abnormalities that inhibit adequate GH secretion, sometimes caused by hypothalamic or pituitary tumors (Figure 3.1). Low plasma IGF-1 concentrations are also caused by acid-labile subunit (ALS) deficiency, hepatic insufficiency, malnutrition, hypothyroidism, delayed puberty, untreated diabetes mellitus, chronic illness, and glucocorticoid therapy (Backeljauw and Chernausek, 2012). GHR deficiencies are associated with a type of dwarfism (Laron syndrome; LR) in which the GHR can not bind its ligand (type I), or is unable to process ligand binding (type II).

Figure 3.1 GH/IGF-1 axis and growth hormone disorders

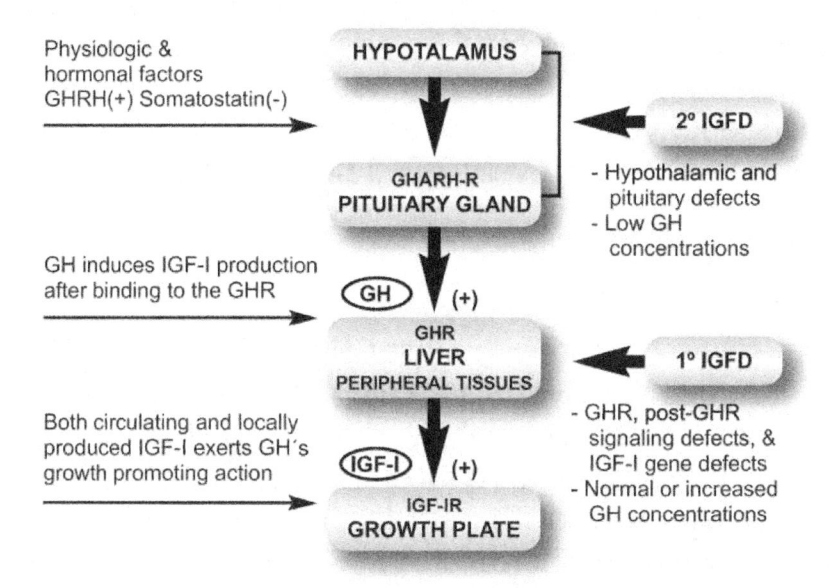

GH: Growth Hormone; **GHR:** Growth Hormone Receptor; **GHRH:** Growth Hormone-Releasing Hormone; **GHRH-R:** Growth Hormone-Releasing Hormone Receptor; **IGF-1:** Insulin-like Growth Factor 1; **IGF-1R:** Insulin-like Growth Factor 1 Receptor; **IGFD:** IGF deficiency.

GH: Growth Hormone; GHR: Growth Hormone Receptor; GHRH: Growth Hormone-Releasing Hormone; GHRH-R: Growth Hormone-Releasing Hormone Receptor; IGF-1: Insulin-like Growth Factor 1; IGF-1R: Insulin-like Growth Factor 1 Receptor; IGFD: IGF deficiency.

Epidemiology

GH deficiency occurs in approximately 1/4,000–1/10,000 children. Although the majority of cases are caused by developmental abnormalities and environmental factors acting on the brain, 3–30 % may be due to genetic mutations (Mullis, 2011). The prevalence of IGF-1 deficiency (IGFD) in short statured, prepubescent children is 20 %. LR affects one in every 2,000 people (Edouard et al., 2009).

Symptoms

Short stature is associated with most GH and IGF deficiencies. Other symptoms include hypoglycemia, immune deficiency, carbohydrate intolerance, deafness, microcephaly, dysmorphic features, body asymmetry and delayed puberty. IGF-1 deficiency can present in utero with intrauterine growth retardation, low weight at birth, as well as severe postnatal short stature.

The statuary growth of children with LR is characterized by relatively normal length at birth, followed by progressive and severe postnatal growth failure. Patients might also present with acromicria, blue sclera, a high pitched voice, limited elbow extension, delayed bone age, hypoglycemia or high cholesterol, facial abnormalities, obesity, delayed puberty or tooth eruption, sparse hair, reduced sweating and thin skin.

Guidelines for GHD diagnosis and management

If a child is not following the predicted, age-appropriate growth curve, underlying illness, genetic disorders, or CNS abnormalities should be considered. GH and IGF-1 serum levels should be measured in short statured children three years or younger. Undetectable IGF-1 levels and increased GH levels might indicate a GH or IGF-1 deficiency. Patients with type I LR may have low GH binding protein (GHBP) levels or have biochemical features similar to patients with classic GH insensitivity, but with normal or increased serum GHBP (type II). Genetic testing can confirm deletions or mutations in candidate genes.

The most recent internationally recognized GHD guidelines are published by The Endocrine Society. They make several recommendations regarding evaluation and treatment (Box3.1).

BOX 3.1: RECOMMENDATIONS FOR GHD DIAGNOSIS

1- The insulin tolerance test (ITT) and the GHRH-arginine test can establish a GHD diagnosis.
2- If the GHRH-arginine test is not available and an ITT is either contraindicated or not practical, the glucagon stimulation test can be used for diagnosis.
3- Pediatric GHD can be caused by irreversible structural lesions, multiple hormone deficiencies, and genetic mutations, low IGF-1 levels at least one month off GH therapy is sufficient documentation of persistent GHD without additional provocative testing.
4- Normal IGF-1 levels do not exclude GHD diagnosis. Low IGF-1 levels, in the absence of catabolic conditions such as poorly controlled diabetes, liver disease, and oral estrogen therapy, is strong evidence for significant GHD. These patients should undergo GH stimulation testing.
5- Deficiencies in three or more pituitary axes strongly suggest the presence of GHD. Under these circumstances, provocative testing is optional.

GH therapy is the treatment most recommended for GHD. It benefits body composition, exercise capacity, and skeletal integrity.

It also improves cardiovascular outcomes. The American Association of Clinical Endocrinologists (AACE) Clinical Guidelines for GH Therapy outline several recommendations when interpreting GH and IGF-1 levels and considering treatment (Figure 3.2) (Cook et al., 2009).

Figure 3.2 Growth hormone therapy recommendations

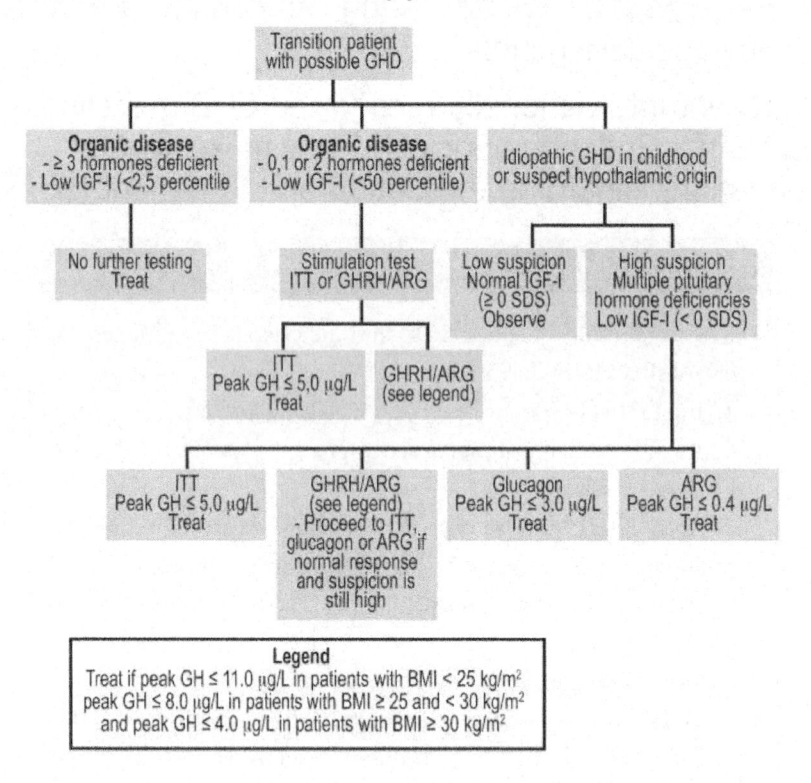

BMI: Body Mass Index; GH: Growth Hormone; GHRH/ARG: Growth Hormone-Releasing Hormone-Arginine test; IGF-1: Insulin-like Growth Factor 1; ITT: Insulin Tolerance Test.

The guidelines recommend that GH therapy be continued after completion of adult height to obtain full skeletal/muscle maturation during the transition period (The Endocrine Society, 2011). Recommendations for GH therapy regimens in adults are listed in Box 3.2 and National Institute for Clinical Health and Excellence

(NICE) Recommendations for GH Therapy regimens in children are listed in Box 3.3 (NICE, 2010).

BOX 3.2: RECOMMENDATIONS FOR GH THERAPY IN ADULTS

1- GH dosing regimens should be individualized rather than weight-based. Therapy should start with lose doses and be titrated according to clinical response, side effects, and IGF-1 levels.
2- Gender, estrogen status, and age should be considered when determining dosage.
3- Patients should be monitored at 1- to 2-month intervals during dose titration and semiannually thereafter with a clinical assessment and evaluation for adverse effects, IGF-1 levels, and other parameters of GH response.

BOX 3.3: RECOMMENDATIONS FOR GH THERAPY IN CHILDREN

1- GH therapy is recommended for children with growth failure associated with: GHD, Turner syndrome, Prader–Willi syndrome, chronic renal insufficiency, born small for gestational age with subsequent growth failure at 4 years of age or later and short stature homeobox (SHOX) deficiency.
2- GH therapies should always be initiated and monitored by a pediatric specialist. The choice of product should be made on an individual basis after informed discussion between the responsible clinician and the caregiver. Therapeutic need and likelihood of treatment adherence should also be considered. If many possible products exist, the least costly product should be chosen.
3- GH therapy should be discontinued if: growth velocity increases less than 50 % from baseline in the first year, final height is approached and growth velocity is less than 2 cm total growth in 1 year, there are insurmountable problems with adherence, or final height is attained. The decision to stop treatment should be discussed with the child's caregiver and the specialist.

Recombinant human IGF-1 therapy is recommended for patients with LR. Frequent meals to avoid hypoglycemia and regular monitoring of glucose plasma levels are suggested. In addition, patients should be regularly monitored for growth and development.

Prognosis

Prompt diagnosis and treatment of growth disorders usually results in good prognosis and reversal of some symptoms. Varying success depends on birth weight, age, and/or height at the start of treatment, extent of the GH or IGF-1 deficiency, duration of treatment, frequency of growth hormone injections, and height at the start of puberty.

Special concerns

GH therapy is not recommended for patients diagnosed with malignant hypothalamic or pituitary tumors. GH treatment in patients with diabetes mellitus (DM) may require adjustments in anti-diabetic medications, and insulin resistance has been observed in patients receiving GH therapy. Thyroid and adrenal function should be monitored during GH therapy. Lastly, prolonged GH therapy is associated with an increased risk for breast cancer in women, and GH and IGF-1 can induce tumor growth. GH therapy must be considered along with anticipated risks and benefits.

People with LR may experience seizures because of low plasma glucose levels, osteopenia and bone fractures. If treating LR patients with IGF-1, they should be closely monitored for adverse effects.

Acromegaly

Acromegaly is characterized by pituitary GH overproduction and secretion, and elevated IGF-1 levels. It usually occurs during middle age and is caused by hypothalamic or pituitary tumors (Ribeiro-Oliveira and Barkan, 2012).

Epidemiology

A recent study estimates acromegaly at 400–1000 cases per million (Ribeiro-Oliveira and Barkan, 2012).

Symptoms

Patients with acromegaly present with acral enlargement. Headaches, loss of vision, sweating, impotence and changes in menstrual cycle may also be associated with the disorder.

Guidelines for acromegaly diagnosis and management

The most recent internationally recognized guidelines for acromegaly management were published in 2010 by the Acromegaly Consensus Group. The guidelines recommend measuring GH and IGF-1 levels to accurately diagnose, manage, and monitor acromegaly (Box 3.4). MRI may be used to detect hypothalamic or pituitary tumors (Giustina et al., 2010).

> **BOX 3.4: ACROMEGALY DIAGNOSIS AND TREATMENT**
>
> 1- Diagnosis can be made if IGF-1 concentrations are elevated, and a failure to suppress GH during an oral glucose tolerance test (OGTT) is noted.
> 2- After neurosurgery or radiotherapy, controlled GH status should be defined as GH suppression during an OGTT for patients not receiving medical therapy, and normal IGF-1 levels should be attained three to six months post-surgery.
> 3- When GH and IGF-1 values are inconsistent; use multiple GH sampling (three to five times over 2 h). For patients receiving somatostatin receptor ligand (SRL) or dopamine agonist therapies, IGF-1 and random GH measurements are sufficient for assessment. In patients receiving a GH receptor antagonist, only IGF-1 should be measured.

The Acromegaly Consensus Group's recommendations for interpretation of GH and IGF-1 levels are shown in Figure 3.3

Figure 3.3 Interpretation of GH and IGF-1 levels in acromegaly (Giustina et al., 2010)

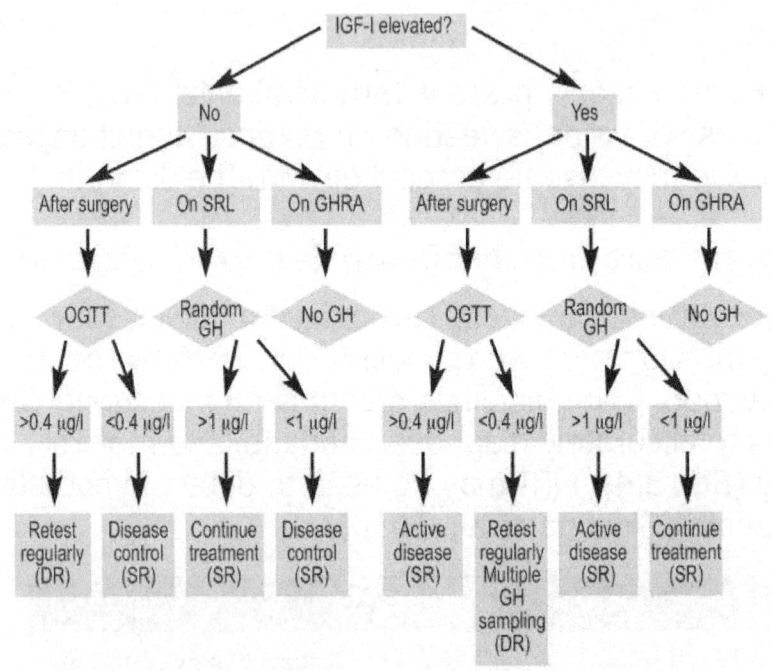

Interpretation of GH and IGF-I levels in acromegaly. GHRA, GH receptor antagonist.

GH: Growth Hormone; GHRA: Growth Hormone Receptor Agonist; OGTT: Oral Glucose Tolerance Test; SRL: Somatostatin Receptor Ligand.

Prognosis

The mortality rate for people with acromegaly is 2–3 times that of the general population, but this may be countered with therapy that normalizes IGF-1 levels. Mortality is associated with cardiovascular and respiratory complications, as well as those associated with DM (Giustina et al., 2010).

Special concerns

When treating patients with acromegaly, use of oral estrogens (not transdermal estrogens) reduces IGF-1 concentrations.

Pancreatic disorders

The pancreatic endocrine function controls glucose metabolism by secreting the hormones INS and glucagon. People who are incapable of producing or making proper use of INS develop DM.

DM-overview

DM is a chronic disease defined by hyperglycemia. Hypoglycemia can occur when the pancreas does not produce enough INS, or when the body is unable to use the INS it produces. DM is classified into three different types. Type 1 diabetes (T1D) is also called INS–dependent, immune-mediated or juvenile-onset diabetes. T1D is an autoimmune disease in which the immune system targets pancreatic β cells, resulting in very little or no INS production. Type 2 diabetes (T2D) is defined by INS resistance and INS deficiency. Gestational diabetes occurs during pregnancy and can cause antepartum and postpartum complications. Several subtypes of diabetes also exist: latent autoimmune diabetes in adults, glucokinase-maturity-onset diabetes of the young, HNF1A-Maturity-onset diabetes of the young, mitochondrial diabetes, lipodystrophies, and neonatal diabetes.

Epidemiology

The World Health Organization (WHO) estimates worldwide DM prevalence at 347 million people. At least 90 % of diabetic people have T2D, and onset usually occurs after 40 years. T1D roughly represents 10 % of diabetics at all ages, particularly children and young adults. Approximately 4 % of pregnant women develop gestational diabetes.

Symptoms

Classical DM symptoms include fatigue, polyuria, extreme thirst despite taking fluids, severe hunger urges, and unexplained weight loss. Others signs may include lack of interest and concentration, nausea and stomach pain, tingling sensations or numbness in hands or feet, blurred vision, frequent infections, and slow-healing wounds.

Guidelines for DM diagnosis and treatment

Using WHO-developed criteria, the International Diabetes Federation (IDF) published 2012 guidelines that provide recommendations on DM diagnosis. Risk assessment should be determined using a questionnaire and high-risk individuals should undergo the glycemic analyses listed in Box 3.5. Asymptomatic individuals with a single abnormal test should have the test repeated to confirm diagnosis unless the result is unequivocally elevated (The International Diabetes Foundation, 2012).

BOX 3.5: GLYCEMIC MEASUREMENTS AND DM DIAGNOSIS IN HIGH RISK INDIVIDUALS

1. Fasting plasma glucose (FPG) ≥ 7.0 mmol/l (126 mg/dl).
2. OGTT 75 g with FPG ≥ 7.0 mmol/l (126 mg/dl) and/or 2 hour plasma glucose ≥ 11.1 mmol/l (200 mg/dl).
3. Glycated hemoglobin (HbA1c) ≥ 6.5 % /48 mmol/mol.
4. Random plasma glucose ≥ 11.1 mmol/l (200 mg/dl) in the presence of classical diabetes symptoms. Where a random plasma glucose level ≥ 5.6 mmol/l (≥ 100 mg/dl) and < 11.1 mmol/l (< 200 mg/dl) is detected, a FPG should be measured, or an OGTT performed, or an HbA1c measured.

DM management involves monitoring plasma glucose levels and managing blood pressure. Early detection of complications is important, and feet and eyes should also be checked regularly. Patients need to be assessed for risk of cardiovascular and kidney disease. Lastly, the IDF recommends for lifestyle management for DM patients, especially those diagnosed with T2D (Box 3.6).

> **BOX 3.6: LIFESTYLE MANAGEMENT FOR PATIENTS WITH DIABETES**
>
> 1. Offer lifestyle advice at diagnosis and review lifestyle modification yearly, at any change in treatment, or as needed.
> 2. Review and provide ongoing counseling and assessment yearly, as needed, or when changes in medication are made.
> 3. Advise people with T2D that lifestyle modifications can be effective in controlling adverse risk factors associated with disorder.
> 4. Provide access to a nutritionist or other health-care professional trained in the principles of nutrition, offering an initial consultation with follow-up sessions as required.
> 5. Individualize advice on meals to match needs, preferences, and culture.
> 6. Advise on reducing energy intake and control of foods with high amounts of added sugars, fats, or alcohol.
> 7. Match timing of medication (including INS treatment for TD1 patients) with meals.
> 8. Provide advice on the use of foods in the prevention and management of hypoglycemia.
> 9. Introduce physical activity gradually, based on the individual's willingness, ability, needs, and goals.
> 10. Encourage increased duration and frequency of physical activity, up to 30-45 minutes 3-5 days per week, or an accumulation of 150 minutes per week of moderate-intensity aerobic activity (50–70 % of maximum heart rate).
> 11. In the absence of contraindications, encourage resistance training three times per week.
> 12. Provide guidance for adjusting medications (e.g. INS) and/or adding carbohydrates for physical activity.

People living with T1D require INS, and INS requirements may change according to age, weight, diet, activity levels and health status. Different types of INS treatment and regimens exist, but should be tailored to meet a patient's needs.

Prognosis

There is no cure for DM. The disease is associated with reduced life expectancy, significant morbidity, and diminished quality of life. It can increase the risk of microvascular damage including retinopathy, nephropathy and neuropathy. It also increases risk of macrovascular complications including ischemic heart disease, stroke and peripheral vascular disease. Prognosis is dependent upon type, blood glucose control, and the occurrence of complications. One third of children diagnosed with T1D develop kidney disease, and people with T2D are five times more likely to develop cardiovascular disease. Lastly, women with gestational diabetes are at higher risk for developing T2D later in life.

Special concerns

Without proper management, people with DM can attain very high plasma glucose levels which can result in long term damage to various organs and tissues. Diabetic nephropathy can result in total kidney failure, and dialysis or kidney transplant might be necessary. Diabetic neuropathy can lead to ulceration and amputation of lower extremities. Diabetic retinopathy is defined by damage to the retina and possible loss of vision. Neonates born from mothers with gestational diabetes are often large for their gestational age. Use of tobacco products is associated with a greater number of disease complications.

Obesity-overview

WHO defines obesity as abnormal or excessive fat accumulation that presents a health risk. Obesity is not an endocrine disorder, but because it is a major etiological factor of T2D, obesity is included in pancreatic dysfunction discussions. It is a chronic disease that is multi-faceted. Causality may lie in genetic behavioral, socio-economic, and environmental factors. Obesity is largely measured by calculating body mass index (BMI; Table 3.1). It is a person's weight (in kilograms) divided by the square of their height in meters.

Category	BMI, kg/m²
Underweight	<18.5
Healthy weight	18.5-24.9
Pre-obese state	25.0-29.9
Obesity grade I	30.0-34.9
Obesity grade II	35.0-39.9
Obesity grade III	≥40

BMI: Body Mass Index

Epidemiology

Overweight and obesity are a global epidemic. In 2008, over 200 million men and nearly 300 million women were estimated to be obese. In 2010, more than 40 million children under the age of five were considered overweight. Overweight and obesity are the fifth leading risk for global deaths. At least 2.8 million adults die each year as a result of being overweight or obese. Obesity is the underlying cause of 44 % of people living with diabetes, and 23 % of people with ischemic heart disease. Overweight and obesity also increase the risk of certain cancer types.

Symptoms

Signs of obesity include the need for larger clothing, weight gain, and an increase in waist circumference. Symptoms include shortness of breath, hyperhidrosis, snoring and difficulty sleeping, an inability to undertake physical activity, fatigue, and back or joint pains.

Guidelines for obesity diagnosis and management

The most recent internationally recognized guidelines on diagnosis and management of obesity are published by the Obesity Management Task Force of the European Association for the Study of Obesity. The guidelines list several recommendations for physical examination, laboratory testing, and diagnosis of an obese patient (Box 3.7; Tsigos et al., 2008).

> **BOX 3.7: RECOMMENDATIONS FOR OBESITY DIAGNOSIS**
>
> 1- Calculate BMI, measure waist circumference, and blood pressure.
> 2- Assess for obesity-related diseases (diabetes, hypertension, dyslipidemia, cardiovascular, respiratory, and joint diseases, non-alcoholic fatty liver disease (NAFLD) and sleep disorders.
> 3- Check for signs of INS resistance (e.g. acanthosis nigricans).
> 4- Minimum laboratory testing should include fasting blood glucose, serum lipid profile (total, HDL and LDL cholesterol, and triglycerides), uric acid, thyroid function, and liver function (hepatic enzymes).
> 5- Cardiovascular assessment.
> 6- Endocrine evaluation if Cushing's syndrome or hypothalamic disease is suspected.
> 7- Liver investigation (ultrasound, biopsy) if abnormal liver function tests suggest NAFLD or other liver pathology.

The 2008 Management of Obesity in Adults: European Clinical Practice Guidelines stress that management and treatment include weight loss (5–10 % of initial body weight), risk reduction, and improved health status through dietary changes and increased physical activity. Management may also include pharmacotherapy and bariatric surgery (Figure 3.4).

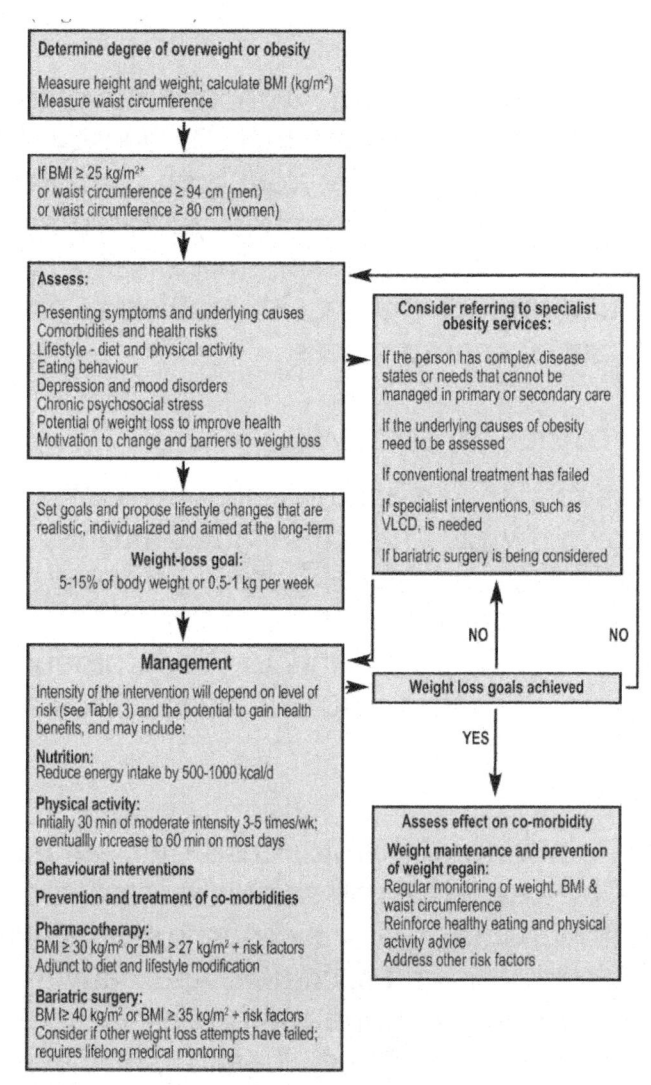

```
┌─────────────────────────────────────┐
│ Determine degree of overweight or obesity │
│                                     │
│ Measure height and weight; calculate BMI (kg/m²) │
│ Measure waist circumference         │
└─────────────────────────────────────┘
                  ↓
┌─────────────────────────────────────┐
│ If BMI ≥ 25 kg/m²*                  │
│ or waist circumference ≥ 94 cm (men) │
│ or waist circumference ≥ 80 cm (women) │
└─────────────────────────────────────┘
                  ↓
┌─────────────────────────────────────┐         ┌─────────────────────────────────┐
│ Assess:                             │         │ Consider referring to specialist │
│                                     │         │       obesity services:         │
│ Presenting symptoms and underlying causes │   │                                 │
│ Comorbidities and health risks      │────────▶│ If the person has complex disease│
│ Lifestyle - diet and physical activity │      │ states or needs that cannot be  │
│ Eating behaviour                    │         │ managed in primary or secondary care │
│ Depression and mood disorders       │         │                                 │
│ Chronic psychosocial stress         │         │ If the underlying causes of obesity │
│ Potential of weight loss to improve health │  │ need to be assessed             │
│ Motivation to change and barriers to weight loss │ │                           │
└─────────────────────────────────────┘         │ If conventional treatment has failed │
                  ↓                             │                                 │
┌─────────────────────────────────────┐         │ If specialist interventions, such as │
│ Set goals and propose lifestyle changes that are │ │ VLCD, is needed          │
│ realistic, individualized and aimed at the long-term │ │                      │
│                                     │         │ If bariatric surgery is being considered │
│        Weight-loss goal:            │         └─────────────────────────────────┘
│ 5-15% of body weight or 0.5-1 kg per week │                    ↑
└─────────────────────────────────────┘                    NO         NO
                  ↓                                         ↑          ↑
┌─────────────────────────────────────┐         ┌─────────────────────────────────┐
│              Management             │────────▶│    Weight loss goals achieved   │
│ Intensity of the intervention will depend on level of │ └─────────────────────────────────┘
│ risk (see Table 3) and the potential to gain health │              YES
│ benefits, and may include:          │                          ↓
│                                     │         ┌─────────────────────────────────┐
│ Nutrition:                          │         │   Assess effect on co-morbidity │
│ Reduce energy intake by 500-1000 kcal/d │     │                                 │
│                                     │         │ Weight maintenance and prevention │
│ Physical activity:                  │         │        of weight regain:        │
│ Initially 30 min of moderate intensity 3-5 times/wk; │ │ Regular monitoring of weight, BMI & │
│ eventually increase to 60 min on most days │  │ waist circumference             │
│                                     │         │ Reinforce healthy eating and physical │
│ Behavioural interventions           │         │ activity advice                 │
│                                     │         │ Address other risk factors      │
│ Prevention and treatment of co-morbidities │  └─────────────────────────────────┘
│                                     │
│ Pharmacotherapy:                    │
│ BMI ≥ 30 kg/m² or BMI ≥ 27 kg/m² + risk factors │
│ Adjunct to diet and lifestyle modification │
│                                     │
│ Bariatric surgery:                  │
│ BMI ≥ 40 kg/m² or BMI ≥ 35 kg/m² + risk factors │
│ Consider if other weight loss attempts have failed; │
│ requires lifelong medical monitoring │
└─────────────────────────────────────┘
```

BMI: Body Mass Index; **VLCD:** Very Low Calorie Diet.

Prognosis

Obesity is preventable. Prognosis depends on successful weight loss and lifelong management. Without proper intervention and management, obesity increases morbidity, disability, mortality and diminishes quality of life.

Special concerns

Obesity and T2D are closely linked. Without intervention and proper management, obesity can develop into T2D. Obesity is also associated with increased mortality from both cardiovascular diseases and certain cancers. Other obesity-related health risks include metabolic complications, respiratory disease, osteoarthritis, gastrointestinal and reproductive health problems, incontinence, and psychological or social consequences.

Thyroid Disorders-overview

Thyroid disorders result from anatomical abnormalities or endocrine dysfunction. Known thyroid anatomical abnormalities include goitre, thyroglossal duct cysts, and lingual (ectopic) thyroid. Hyperthyroidism is caused by overproduction and secretion of the thyroid hormones TSH, TRH, T3, and T4. Underproduction or under-secretion of thyroid hormones results in hypothyroidism.

Hyperthyroidism

Hyperthyroidism is a form of thyrotoxicosis that can develop several different ways. The thyroid can be stimulated into secreting hormones by nutritional factors or by constitutive activation of thyroid hormone synthesis and secretion. Alternatively, thyroid stores of pre-synthesized hormone can be passively released because of autoimmune, infectious, chemical, or mechanical triggers. Lastly, overproduction or oversecretion can result from exposure to thyroid hormone sources outside of the thyroid. The most common causes of hyperthyroidism include Graves' disease (GD), toxic multi-nodular goiter, and toxic adenoma. GD is an autoimmune disease in which thyrotropin receptor antibodies stimulate the TSH receptor, increasing thyroid hormone production (Bahn et al., 2011).

Epidemiology

Approximately 1.2 % of the general population has hyperthyroidism. Subclinical hyperthyroidism represents 0.7 %, and overt (or clinical) hyperthyroidism is responsible for the remaining 0.5 %. Prevalence may increase to 3 % in elderly population. Approximately 0.2 % of pregnant women have hyperthyroidism.

Symptoms

Hyperthyroidism symptoms include poor weight gain despite an increase in appetite, tachycardia or arrhythmia, hypertension, nervousness, irritability, difficulty sleeping, bulging eyes, vomiting, diarrhea, dyspnea, heat intolerance, and moist skin. Women may report the cessation of periods. Some patients may present with a bulge in the neck due to an enlarged thyroid gland (goitre).

Guidelines for hyperthyroidism diagnosis and management

Overt (or clinical) hyperthyroidism is characterized by excess thyroid hormones in serum and suppressed TSH (<0.01 mU/l). There are also measurable changes in basal metabolic rate, cardiovascular hemodynamics, and psychiatric and neuropsychological function. The most recent internationally recognized guidelines on hypothyroidism management were published in 2011 by the American Thyroid Association and the AACE. In addition to the Hyperthyroidism Symptom Scale (HSS; Figure 3.5), AACE Hyperthyroidism and Other Causes of Thyrotoxicosis: Management Guidelines recommendations concerning initial evaluation and management of hyperthyroidism are listed in Box 3.8 (Bahn et al., 2011).

Figure 3.5 Hyperthyroidism Symptom Scale (Klein et al., 1988)

A score > 20 is predictive of hyperthyroidism, and < 10 indicates a euthyroid state.

Hyperthyroid Symptom Scale

Characteristic	Score
Nervousness	_____

  0. Absent
  1. Anxious only with stress
  2. Occasionally anxious at rest
  3. Often anxious, difficulty working or concentrating
  4. States freely that feels "very nervous most of the time"

Sweating _____

  0. Only with activity
  1. At rest but only in warm temperatures
  2. At rest in temperate climates, mainly involving the hands and intertriginous zones
  3. At rest involving many body areas
  4. Profusely diaphoratic almost constantly

Heat tolerance _____

  0. Normal temperature tolerance
  1. Periods of feeling warmer than those in the same room
  2. Significant difficulty with heat, requiring air conditioner constantly in the summertime
  3. Excessive difficulty with heat even in temperate climates
  4. Extreme difficulty with heat, does not feel comfortable even in cold weather as evidenced by lack of need for warm clothing or bed covers

Hyperactivity _____

  0. Normal activity level
  1. Increased activity level, increased productivity
  2. Increased productivity; decreased sleep time
  3. Performs some purposeless activity
  4. Frequent episodes of purposeless activity; unable to sit still during examination

Hyperthyroid Symptom Scale	
Characteristic	Score

Tremor: Examination of outstretched hands _____
  0. Absent
  1. Barely perceptible
  2. Tremor demonstrated readily on examination
  3. Marked tremor but able to perform fine motor skills
  4. Hands snake excessively, difficulty performing fine motor skills

Weakness _____
  0. Normal strength
  1. Subjetive weakness but with normal exercise tolerance
  2. Decreased exercise tolerance to near maximal activity
  3. Decreased tolerance to stair climbing or arising from chair
  4. Extreme weakness such that patient can barely lift objects or walk up stairs

Hyperdynamic precordium _____
  0. Normal precordium activity and apical impulse
  1. Tachycardia, 90 beats per minute with normal apical impulse
  2. Tachycardia, 90 beats per minute with increased apical impulse
  3. Tachycardia, 110 beats per minute with increased apical impulse
  4. Tachycardia, 110 beats per minute, apical impulse and carotid upstroke both increased, systolic outflow murmur

Diarrhea _____
  0. 1 bowel movement (BM) per day; formed stool
  1. 2-4 formed BMs per day
  2. 1-4 loose stools per day
  3. 4 formed BMs per day
  4. 4 loose stools per day

Hyperthyroid Symptom Scale	
Characteristic	**Score**
Appetite	_____
0. Appetite normal, no weight loss	
1. Appetite normal, weight loss	
2. Appetite increased, no weight loss	
3. Appetite increased weight loss	
4. Appetite decreased, weight loss	
Assessment of daily function (degree of incapaciation)	_____
0. Normal (none)	
1. Minimal impairment (10%)	
2. Mild impairment (30%)	
3. Moderate impairment (60%)	
4. Severe impairment (90%)	
	Total Score _____

> **BOX 3.8: EVALUATION AND INITIAL MANAGEMENT OF HYPERTHYROIDISM**
>
> 1- Severity of hyperthyroidism should be assessed according to the HSS.
> 2- All patients with known or suspected hyperthyroidism should undergo a comprehensive history and physical examination, including measurement of pulse rate, blood pressure, respiratory rate, and body weight.
> 3- The thyroid should be checked for abnormalities i.e. size, pain or absence of pain, symmetry, and nodularity. Pulmonary, cardiac, and neuromuscular function, and presence or absence of peripheral edema, eye signs, or pretibial myxedema should be assessed.
> 4- Diagnostic accuracy improves when both serum TSH and free T4 are assessed. In overt hyperthyroidism, usually both serum free T4 and T3 estimates are elevated, and serum TSH is undetectable. In milder hyperthyroidism, serum T4 and free T4 estimates can be normal, only serum T3 may be elevated, and serum TSH will be <0.01mU/l.
> 5- To determine etiology, a radioactive iodine uptake test should be performed when the clinical presentation of thyrotoxicosis is not diagnostic of GD. A thyroid scan should be added in the presence of thyroid nodularity.
> 6- Initiation of treatment should be based on etiology.
> 7- Antithyroid medications including beta-adrenergic blockade should be considered in all patients with symptomatic thyrotoxicosis. Beta-adrenergic blockade should be given to elderly patients with symptomatic thyrotoxicosis and to other thyrotoxic patients with resting heart rates in excess of 90 bpm or coexistent cardiovascular disease.
> 8- Patients with GD should be treated with ^{131}I therapy, antithyroid medication, or thyroidectomy.
> 9- If ^{131}I therapy is chosen, sufficient radiation should be administered in a single dose (10–15 mCi) to render the patient hypothyroid. The physician administering the therapy should provide written information concerning radiation safety precautions following treatment. If the precautions cannot be followed, alternative therapy should be selected.

Prognosis

Hyperthyroidism is usually treatable and antithyroid drugs can be very effective depending on etiology. Most patients that undergo 131I therapy respond to radioactive iodine and have normal thyroid function tests and clinical symptoms within 4–8 weeks. If hyperthyroidism persists in GD patients after 6 months, or if there is minimal response after 3 months, the AACE guidelines recommend retreatment.

Special concerns

Untreated hyperthyroidism or thyrotoxicosis can lead to osteoporosis, atrial fibrillation, embolic events, cardiovascular collapse, and death. Treating hyperthyroidism with 131I therapy is contraindicated in pregnant or lactating women, as well as women planning conception within 4–6 months. Patients with coexisting or suspected thyroid cancer, or individuals unable to comply with radiation safety guidelines should not undergo 131I therapy. The benefits and risks of surgery should be weighed in patients with cardiopulmonary disease, end-stage cancer, or other debilitating disorders.

Hypothyroidism

Subclinical hypothyroidism is defined by a serum TSH level above the upper reference limit in combination with a normal free T4. This is only applicable when thyroid function is stable, the hypothalamic–pituitary–thyroid axis is normal, and there is no recent or ongoing severe illness. Overt hypothyroidism is defined by elevated TSH concentration (>10 UI/l) in combination with subnormal T4 levels (Garber et al., 2012). It is further classified into three types. Primary hyperthyroidism is defined by normal TSH levels but nonexistent T3 or T4 levels, usually caused by a dysfunctional thyroid gland. Secondary hypothyroidism is caused by impaired pituitary function in which inadequate amounts of TSH are produced and secreted. Tertiary hypothyroidism results from impaired hypothalamic function, in which inadequate levels of TRH are secreted. The most common cause of hypothyroidism is environmental iodine deficiency, but autoimmune thyroid diseases and radioiodine (used in the treatment of hyperthyroidism) are also causative factors.

Epidemiology

Subclinical hypothyroidism occurs in 8 % of women and 3 % of men. Overt hypothyroidism occurs in 1–2 % of women and 0.9 % of men. Prevalence for both types increase with age. During pregnancy, 3–5 % of women develop subclinical hypothyroidism and 0.3–0.5 % of women develop overt hypothyroidism. For those people that develop overt hypothyroidism, the majority are cases of primary hypothyroidism. Only 5–10 % of these are secondary and 5 % are tertiary forms of the disorder. Congenital hypothyroidism occurs once in every 4,000 births.

Symptoms

Hypothyroidism symptoms usually include dry skin, cold sensitivity, fatigue, muscle cramps, voice changes, and constipation. Other less common symptoms may include carpal tunnel syndrome, sleep apnea, and pituitary hyperplasia with or without hyperprolactinemia and galactorrhea, as well as hyponatremia (Garber et al., 2012).

Guidelines for hypothyroidism diagnosis and management

Although age contributes to hypothyroidism, no consensus has been reached on how old a patient should be to be considered for a hypothyroidism evaluation. However, many health agencies that recommend individuals with any of the medical conditions listed in Box 3.9 be tested.

> **BOX 3.9: MEDICAL EVIDENCE THAT CAN PROMPT HYPOTHYROIDISM SCREENING**
>
> - Autoimmune disease including T1D
> - Pernicious anemia
> - First-degree relative with autoimmune thyroid disease
> - History of neck radiation to the thyroid gland (^{131}I therapy for hyperthyroidism) and external beam radiotherapy for head and neck malignancies
> - Prior history of thyroid surgery or dysfunction
> - Abnormal thyroid examination
> - Psychiatric disorders
> - Patients taking amiodarone or lithium
> - Adrenal insufficiency
> - Alopecia
> - Anemia
> - Cardiac dysrhythmia, hypertension, congestive heart failure, prolonged QT interval
> - Skin texture changes or vitiligo
> - Constipation
> - Dysmenorrhea
> - Hypercholesterolemia and mixed hyperlipidemia
> - Malaise and fatigue
> - Myopathy
> - Excessive weight gain

According to the AACE Clinical Practice Guidelines for Hypothyroidism in Adults, measuring serum TSH concentration is the primary screening test for thyroid dysfunction. The AACE recommends routine TSH measurement in older patients, especially women. It is also used for monitoring effectiveness of thyroid hormone replacement therapy in primary hypothyroidism patients or those with thyroid cancer. The upper normal range of serum TSH levels is 4.5 mIU/l. Measuring serum free T4 is the primary test for detecting hypothyroidism in antithyroid drug–treated, surgical, or radioiodine-treated hyperthyroidism patients in whom serum TSH may remain low for many weeks to months (Garber et al., 2012).

The ACCE recommends L-thyroxine monotherapy for patients with primary hypothyroidism as the benefits of L-thyroxine and L-triiodothyronine combination therapy have not been proven. The daily recommended dosage is approximately 1.6 μg/kg, but it may also depend on age, sex, and body size. Only serum TSH levels within the normal range should determine therapeutic endpoint. Measuring free T4 and T3 levels alone or clinical indicators are insufficient in this situation.

Prognosis

Even if left untreated, patients with hypothyroidism can function without complications for an extended period of time. If treated with L-thyroxine, however, treatment endpoint should be when TSH values return to the normal range. Prolonged treatment can cause cardiac hypertrophy and arrhythmias. A small percentage of patients may develop myxedema coma, in a severe, longstanding deficiency of serum thyroid hormones that results in loss of brain function.

Special concerns

TSH levels vary diurnally. Values are lowest in the late afternoon and highest when the patient is asleep. Very mild TSH elevations in older individuals may not necessarily reflect subclinical thyroid dysfunction, but rather be a sign of aging.

Although most physicians can readily diagnose hypothyroidism, the ACCE recommends referral to an endocrinologist for situations listed in Box 3.10 (Garber et al., 2012).

> **BOX 3.10: SPECIAL CONCERNS FOR HYPOTHYROIDISM**
>
> 1. If hypothyroidism is indicated in infants and children.
> 2. Patients in whom it is difficult to render and maintain a euthyroid state
> 3. Pregnancy or women planning conception
> 4. Cardiac disease
> 5. Presence of goiter, nodule, or other structural changes in the thyroid gland
> 6. Presence of other endocrine disease such as adrenal and pituitary disorders
> 7. Unusual constellation of thyroid function test results

Parathyroid disorders-overview

Parathyroid disorders arise from abnormal levels of parathyroid hormone that interfere with calcium metabolism. Vitamin D deficiency is also linked to parathyroid disorders as vitamin D facilitates calcium absorption in the gastrointestinal tract. Abnormal serum calcium levels trigger or inhibit PTH synthesis and secretion, affecting bone resorption and urinary phosphate excretion. Thus, parathyroid dysfunction and disease results from PTH excess or deficiency that presents in the form of hypercalcemia or hypocalcemia, ultimately impairing the musculoskeletal and cardiovascular systems.

Hyperparathyroidism

Hyperparathyroidism (also known as parathyroid disease) is characterized by elevated PTH levels secreted from one or more enlarged glands. Constitutively high levels of PTH increase serum calcium levels by hijacking the skeletal system, possibly leading to osteopenia and osteoporosis. Patients with normocalcemic hyperparathyroidism have elevated PTH and normal serum calcium levels. Primary hyperparathyroidism is often caused by a parathyroid adenoma or multi-glandular parathyroid disease. Disease-causing adenomas can also be found outside of the parathyroid glands in the thyroid, thymus, trachea-esophageal groove, and mediastinum. Rarely, hyperparathyroidism is caused by one or multiple parathyroid carcinoma tumors. Secondary hyperparathyroidism can result from inadequate renal failure (Westin et al., 2009). Dysfunctional kidneys are unable to produce sufficient vitamin D or excrete phosphorus. This leads to low calcium levels and stimulation of the parathyroid glands to overproduce PTH.

Epidemiology

The approximate prevalence of hyperparathyroidism is 28 people per 100,000. It is twice as common in women, and prevalence increases with age. Approximately 85 % of cases are caused by a single adenoma of parathyroid chief cells. Multi-glandular parathyroid hyperplasia occurs in 1–15 % of hyperparathyroidism patients, and parathyroid carcinoma is responsible for less than 1 % of cases.

Symptoms

Hyperparathyroidism is often asymptomatic, and may only become apparent when abnormal serum or bone calcium levels cause dysfunction in other organs or systems. Symptoms, if any, might include osteoporosis or joint pain, kidney stones, polyuria, abdominal pain, fatigue or malaise, depression, nausea or vomiting, and loss of appetite.

Guidelines for hyperparathyroidism diagnosis and management

An international committee published the Guidelines for the Management of Asymptomatic Primary Hyperparathyroidism in 2009. The guidelines recommend that all patients biochemically diagnosed with primary hyperparathyroidism and showing signs of disease should undergo surgery. Threshold values for serum calcium and other measurements are listed in Table 3.2. Hypercalciuria alone (i.e. in the absence of renal stones or nephrolithiasis) is no longer considered an indication for parathyroid surgery.

Table 3.2 Threshold values for patients with asymptomatic primary hyperparathyroidism (modified from Bilezekian et al., 2009)

Measurement	Threshold value
Serum calcium (> upper limit of normal)	1.0 mg/dl (0.25 mmol/l)
24 h urinary calcium	No consensus (some physicians consider > 400 mg as an indication for surgery)
Calculated creatinine clearance	Reduced to < 60 ml/min
Bone mineral density	T-score < -2.5 at any site and/or previous fracture fragility
Age (years)	< 50

If parathyroidectomy is contraindicated or not chosen, pharmacotherapy with bisphosphonates, estrogen replacement, and calcimimetic drugs can reduce serum calcium and PTH levels. The guidelines recommend close monitoring of several parameters of these patients (Table 3.3).

Table 3.3 Management guidelines for monitoring patients that do not undergo parathyroidectomy

Measurement	Frequency
Serum calcium	Annually
24 h urinary calcium	Not recommended
Creatinine clearance (24-h urine collections)	Not recommended
Serum creatinine	Not recommended
Bone density	Every 1–2 yr (3 sites) or as needed
Abdominal x-ray (ultrasound)	Annually

Treatment of patients with secondary hyperparathyroidism depends on etiology. Vitamin D deficiency can be treated with calcitriol. Patients with renal failure must undergo kidney transplantation and can also be administered bisphosphonates, calcitriol, and calcimimetics.

Prognosis

Hyperparathyroidism is a progressive disease unless cured by parathyroidectomy, which has a success rate of ≥ 95 % for a single adenoma. Bone density may improve after tumors are removed, depending on severity of bone deterioration. However, damage incurred (if any) by the pancreas or kidneys may be permanent. Apart from complications due to renal failure, secondary hyperparathyroidism patients can develop calciphylaxis that can cause skin lesions, necrosis and ulcers.

Special concerns

Primary hyperparathyroidism patients that do not undergo parathyroidectomy need to be closely monitored. In addition, osteoporosis increases the risk of fractures. Not all secondary hyperparathyroidism patients respond to medication and are at high risk of disease reoccurrence.

Hypoparathyroidism

Hypoparathyroidism is characterized by low levels of serum PTH and hypocalcaemia. Pseudohypoparathyroidism is defined by both of these characteristics and resistance to parathyroid hormone. The former ranges from asymptomatic and only identified through a biochemical test, to life-threatening disease. Hypoparathyroidism is most often caused by autoimmune disorders. It may also result from thyroidectomy, parathyroidectomy, and 131I therapy for hyperparathyroidism. Iron overload in thalassemia patients is another common cause, as well as genetically inherited mutations in PTH signaling factors and calcium sensing pathways including DiGeorge syndrome or Sanjad–Sakati syndrome.

Epidemiology

Transient hypoparathyroidism occurs in approximately 10 % of thyroidectomy patients, and 4.4 % of patients still have the disorder after 6 months. Hypoparathyroidism prevalence with autoimmune dysfunction can range from 1/9, 000 to 1/25, 000. Thalassemia prevalence is higher in warmer climates and can reach 16 %. It is estimated that DiGeorge syndrome occurs once in every 4,000 births and the prevalence of Sanjad-Sakati syndrome is unknown.

Symptoms

Signs and symptoms of hypoparathyroidism vary depending on etiology and severity of the disease. Moreover, symptoms are related to hypocalcemia, and not low serum PTH levels. Acute hypocalcaemia can cause laryngospasm, neuromuscular irritability, cognitive impairment, personality disturbances, prolonged QT intervals, electrocardiographic changes that mimic myocardial infarction, and possible heart failure. Other symptoms may include steatorrhea, cataract formation, circumoral numbness, paresthesias, carpal and pedal muscle spasms, tetany, and seizures (De Sanctis et al., 2012).

Guidelines for hypoparathyroidism diagnosis and management

There are no internationally recognized guidelines that address diagnosis and management of hypoparathyroidism. However, several common laboratory tests may be used to establish a hypoparathyroidism diagnosis (Table 3.4).

Table 3.4 Biochemical analyses used to diagnose hypoparathyroidism (De Sanctis et al., 2012)

Investigations to establish a diagnosis hypoparathyroidism	
Basic investigations	Serum calcium (corrected for albumin or ionized calcium), phosphate, alkaline phosphatise
	Magnesium
	Electrolytes
	Creatinine
	Parathyroid hormone
	Serum pH
	Complete blood count
	25-hydroxyvitamin D
Further investigations	24-h urinary phosphate, calcium and creatinine
	Renal ultrasonography to assess for nephrolithiasis
	DNA sequencing to exclude genetic mutations
	Biochemistry in firs-degree family members

Hypoparathyroidism treatment options currently include calcium, vitamin D metabolites and analogues, thiazide diuretics, bisphosphonates, and low-salt/phosphate diets. Some recommendations for acute hypocalcemia treatment are listed in Box 3.11.

> **BOX 3.11: MANAGEMENT OF ACUTE HYPOCALCAEMIA**
>
> 1. Hypocalcemic patients with or without other symptoms should be hospitalized until diagnostic tests and treatment are initiated. Symptomatic hypocalcaemia patients with serum total calcium level below 7 mg/dl (1.75 mmol/l) should receive intravenous calcium treatment. Serum calcium levels must be measured frequently in this period.
> 2. Intravenous calcium infusion irritates the vein. Good intravenous access should be established to prevent the risk of skin necrosis in the event of extravasation.
> 3. Transition from intravenous therapy to oral therapy is recommended when serum total calcium concentration is in a safe range (>7.5 mg/dl¼1.88 mmol/l).
> 4. Vitamin D supplementation and oral calcium should be initiated as soon as possible. Once serum calcium concentrations range from 8 to 9 mg/dl (2–2.25 mmol/l), the dose should be weaned to maintain a low-to-normal serum calcium concentration.
> 5. Estrogens increase intestinal calcium absorption.

Therapeutic endpoints can be considered when symptoms are controlled, serum calcium levels are in the low to normal range, serum phosphorus levels are within normal limits, 24 h urinary calcium is under 7.5 mmol/day (300 mg/day), and a calcium–phosphate product under 55 mg/dl (4.4 mmol/l) is obtained (De Sanctis et al., 2012).

Prognosis

Early hypoparathyroidism diagnosis reflects good prognosis. Successful treatment of acute hypocalcaemia is more readily accomplished that treating chronic hypocalcaemia. However, damage to teeth, cataract formation, and brain calcifications are irreversible.

Special concerns

Hypoparathyroidism increases excretion of urinary calcium, and vitamin D intoxication can lead to hypercalciuria, nephrolithiasis, and nephrocalcinosis. Tissue calcifications can also occur. Thiazide diuretics are effective in reducing urinary calcium excretion, but loop diuretics can depress serum calcium and should be avoided. Glucocorticoids can interfere with vitamin D action (De Sanctis et al., 2012).

Conclusion

Growth and metabolic disorders affect statuary growth, weight, and development. They can also impair overall metabolism, glucose homoeostasis, and calcium/phosphate metabolism.

Chapter 4: The Reproductive System and Endocrine Disorders

Introduction

Under normal conditions, human reproduction and development are tightly regulated by the endocrine system and the controlled synthesis and secretion of steroid hormones. Reproductive endocrine alterations are a normal part of aging, as seen in menopause and post menopausal status. Male and female endocrine reproductive disorders can arise from an abnormal imbalance between estrogens and androgens, and the etiologies are multi-factorial. Common reproductive endocrine disorders are hirsutism and gynecomastia. Erectile dysfunction can also be caused by endocrine dysfunction.

Menopause and postmenopause-overview

Menopause is characterized by the ovarian decline of estrogen and progesterone synthesis and secretion. The menstrual cycle is eventually halted and this elicits physiological changes in middle aged women. As the egg supply depletes, ovaries no longer respond to pituitary signaling through the gonadotropins FSH and LH, and serum levels of both hormones increase. Thus, the number of ovarian follicles predetermined at birth, determines onset of menopause, gonadotropin levels, and steroid hormone secretion (WHO, 1996). The time periods surrounding menopause are shown in Figures 4.1a and b. Genetics, ethnicity, health status, BMI, lifestyle, and socio-economic factors can also contribute to the natural onset of menopause.

Early menopause can occur in women 45 years or younger. Spontaneous premature menopause is caused by premature ovarian failure (POF), in which the ovarian egg supply has been compromised. POF etiology is multi-factorial. It can be caused by genetic mutations, chromosomal anomalies, surgery, infection, autoimmune disorders, and endocrine dysfunction. This includes abnormal FSH and LH secretion and action, as well as thyroid dysfunction and hypoparathyroidism. Induced menopause can result from oophorectomy, chemotherapy, and radiotherapy.

Figure 4.1a Time periods that surround menopause (WHO, 1996)

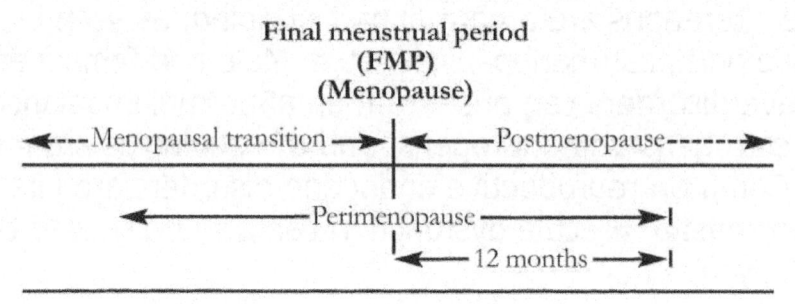

Figure 4.1b Menopause and hormone levels
(http://womensvoicesforchange.org)

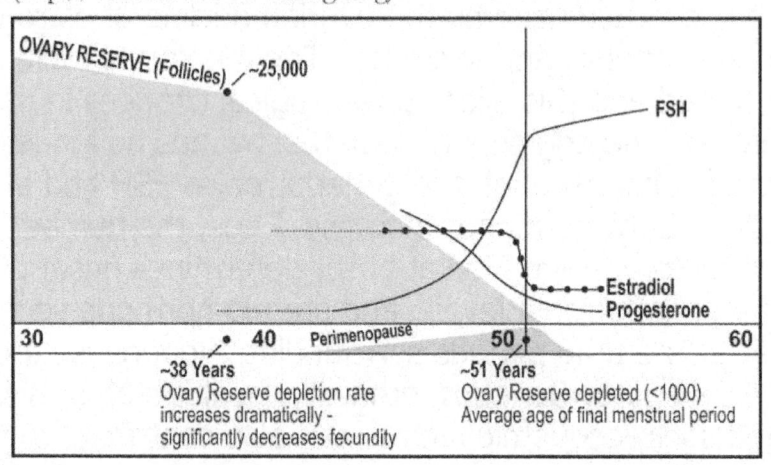

Epidemiology

The progressive decline of estrogen synthesis usually begins for women in their late 30s, completely halting by their mid-50s. The prevalence of women with estrogen deficiency and postmenopausal status depends upon the aging demographic. Spontaneous premature menopause occurs in 1 % of women less than 40 years and 0.1 % of those less than 30 years, although prevalence may vary in different ethnic backgrounds. Early menopause affects approximately 5–10 % women in the general population. The average age of postmenopausal status is 51 years.

Symptoms

Menopause can be asymptomatic. However, approximately 85 % of women undergoing menopause report physiological symptoms that include hot flashes, cold sweats, dizziness, faintness, nausea, vomiting, breast tenderness, bloating, weight gain, skin and hair disorders, anorexia nervosa, edema, swelling, pelvic discomfort, headaches or migraines, changes in bowel habit, and reduced coordination. Psychological symptoms may include mental stress, mood disturbances, panic attacks, depression, irritability, anxiety, insomnia, fatigue, confusion, memory loss, insomnia, distractibility, restlessness, and loneliness.

Guidelines for diagnosis and management of menopause

and postmenopause

There is no definitive test to diagnose the onset and early stages of menopause (perimenopause). However, measuring serum FSH levels may confirm postmenopausal status after the transition period.

The AACE Medical Guidelines for Clinical Practice for the Diagnosis and Treatment of Menopause recommend hormone replacement therapy (HRT) to alleviate symptoms and improve quality of life for menopausal women. It is also indicated for the prevention of osteoporosis in postmenopausal women. HRT consists of estrogen therapy alone or in combination with progesterone therapy. Commonly used medications are listed in table 4.1.

Table 4.1 Common medications for hormone replacement therapy

Hormone	Medication (daily dosage if standardized)
Estrogen	Conjugated equine or synthesized conjugated estrogens (0.3 to 0.625 mg)
	Orally administered micronized 17b-estradiol for oral administration (0.5 to 1 mg) or injection
	Transdermal estradiol (25 to 100 µg)
	Ethinyl estradiol (0.01 to 0.02 mg)
	Topically applied estradiol emulsion, gel, and spray
	Vaginal estrogenic preparations, including a vaginal estradiol ring and creams of conjugated equine estrogen (CEE) and estradiol
Progestagen	Medroxyprogesterone acetate (MPA) (2.5 mg daily or 5 mg for 10 to 12 days/mo)
	Micronized progesterone (100 mg daily or 200 mg for 10 to 12 days/mo)
	Norethindrone acetate (0.35 mg daily or 5 mg for 10 to 12 days/mo)
	Drospirenone (3 mg daily)
	Levonorgestrel (0.075 mg daily)
Combination therapy	Orally administered estradiol-drospirenone
	Orally administered CEE-MPA
	Orally ethinyl estradiol-norethindrone acetate
	Orally administered estradiol-norgestimate
	Transdermal estradiol-levonorgestrel
	Transdermal estradiol-norethindrone acetate

Although HRT is widely recommended, the Food and Drug Administration (FDA) in the Unites States contraindicates the use of

HRT under certain situations. Contraindications are listed in Box. 4.1 (Goodman et al., 2011).

> **BOX 4.1: CONTRAINDICATIONS TO HORMONE REPLACEMENT THERAPY**
>
> 1- Current, past, or suspected breast cancer.
> 2- Known or suspected estrogen-sensitive malignant conditions.
> 3- Undiagnosed genital bleeding.
> 4- Untreated endometrial hyperplasia.
> 5- Previous idiopathic or current venous thromboembolism.
> 6- Active or recent arterial thromboembolic disease.
> 7- Untreated hypertension.
> 8- Active liver disease.
> 9- Hypersensitivity to HRT agents.
> 10- Porphyria cutanea tarda.

A woman is considered postmenopausal when she has not menstruated in 12 months. Measurement of FSH levels can confirm this diagnosis. As with menopause, HRT is also recommended for postmenopausal women. Duration of HRT varies depending on the hormones administered, and extended use may carry certain risks. If estrogen and progestagen combination therapy is administered, there is an increased risk of breast cancer and mortality. Estrogen therapy alone presents a lower risk (NAMS, 2012).

Prognosis

Menopausal and prognosis is variable. Symptoms can usually be treated efficiently with HRT. Symptoms may last from 5–10 years after onset, although in some women menopausal symptoms persistent beyond that time frame. Endocrine changes are permanent. HRT also reduces the severity of symptoms associated with postmenopause. However, postmenopausal status and aging are accompanied by the onset of other chronic illnesses that may include coronary heart disease, stroke, osteoporosis, dementia, and cancer. Thus, mortality and morbidity outcomes rely heavily on associated diseases. Studies have demonstrated that HRT significantly reduces mortality when initiated for women younger than 60 years (NAMS, 2012).

Special concerns

Many side effects to progestagen therapy have been reported, ranging from mild to intolerable premenstrual-tension-like symptoms, including mood swings, bloating, fluid retention, and sleep disturbance. Switching therapies may decrease symptoms. As menopause and postmenopause are both associated with the onset and progression of coronary heart disease, stroke, osteoporosis, dementia, and cancer, the benefits and risks of HRT and comorbidities of these chronic illnesses should be considered (Goodman et al., 2011).

The known risks associated with prolonged HRT have prompted many patients to treat menopause and postmenopause with herbal remedies. Treatment with herbal remedies has yet to be scientifically validated.

Gynecomastia-overview

Gynecomastia is a common disorder characterized by the enlargement of mammary glands in males. It occurs when the balance between estrogen and testosterone is disrupted, and can happen via several physiological or non physiological mechanisms. Physiological gynecomastia has a trimodal age distribution that presents in newborns, adolescents, and men over 50 years. Gynecomastia in neonates results from exposure to maternal estrogens while in utero. During adolescence, more estrogen may be produced by the testes and peripheral tissues before testosterone secretion attains adult male levels. In the older male, free testosterone levels steadily decrease. The testes may also secrete too much estrogen from Leydig cell or Sertoli cell tumors, or pituitary gland tumors may secrete excessive amounts of human chorionic gonadotropin (hCG) or prolactin (Dickson, 2012). Lastly, gynecomastia can arise from primary or secondary hypogonadism.

Hypogonadism occurs when the testes synthesize and secrete inadequate amounts of testosterone. Primary hypogonadism can result from 5α-reductase deficiency, androgen insensitivity syndrome, congenital anorchia, hemochromatosis, Klinefelter syndrome, mumps virus infection, and testicular torsion or trauma. Secondary hypogonadism arises in patients with Kallmann syndrome.

Nonphysiological causes of gynecomastia are characterized by the use of certain medications and substances. Many of the agents associated with onset are listed in Table 4.2.

Table 4.2 Medications and substances associated with gynecomastia

Mechanism	Medication (brand name) or substance
Anti-androgenic	Alkylating agents Bicalutamide (Casodex) Cimetidine (Tagamet) Cisplatin Flutamide Isoniazid Ketoconazole Marijuana Methotrexate Metronidazole (Flagyl) Omeprazole (Prilosec) Penicillamine (Cuprimine) Ranitidine (Zantac) Spironolactone (Aldactone) Vinca alkaloids
Estrogenic	Anabolic steroids Diazepam (Valium) Digoxin Estrogen agonists Estrogens Gonadotropin-releasing hormone agonists Human chorionic gonadotropins Phenytoin (Dilantin) Phytoestrogens
Increased androgen metabolism	Alcohol
Increased sex hormone-binding globulin concentration	Diazepam Phenytoin
Induced hyperprolactinemia	Haloperidol Metoclopramide (Reglan) Phenothiazines

Mechanism	Medication (brand name) or substance
Unknown	Amiodarone Amlodipine (Norvasc) Amphetamines Angiotensin-converting enzyme inhibitors Antiretroviral agents Atorvastatin (Lipitor) Didanosine (Videx) Diltiazem Etomidate (Amidate) Fenofibrate (Tricor) Finasteride Fluoxetine (Prozac) Heroin Methadone Methyldopa Minocycline (Minocin) Minoxidil Mirtazapine (Remeron) Nifedipine (Procardia) Nilutamide (Nilandron) Paroxetine (Paxil) Reserpine Risperidone (Risperdal) Rosuvastatin (Crestor) Sulindac (Clinoril) Theophylline Tricyclic antidepressants Venlafaxine (Effexor) Verapamil

Epidemiology

The prevalence of physiological gynecomastia is 60–90 % in neonates, 50–60 % in adolescents, and up to 70 % in males aged 50 to 69 years. Approximately 25 % percent of all gynecomastia cases are physiological, another 25 % are idiopathic, and 10-25 % of cases are caused by medication or substance use. Primary hypogonadism (8 %), secondary hypogonadism (2 %), tumors 3 %, hypothyroidism 3 %, chronic renal insufficiency (1 %) and other causes (6 %; familial gynecomastia, HIV, malnutrition, impaired intestinal absorption) are responsible for the remaining cases (Dickson, 2012).

Symptoms

Apart from breast enlargement, gynecomastia is often asymptomatic. Patients with symptomatic gynecomastia may present with palpable masses under the nipples or one or both sides of the chest, breast tenderness or pain, and/or nipple discharge. Other symptoms may include testicular masses, decreased libido, ED, changes in testicle size, weight gain, or weight loss.

Guidelines for gynecomastia diagnosis and management

Internationally recognized guidelines on the evaluation and management of gynecomastia are not yet available. However, the Mayo Clinic Proceedings from the United States recommend that a thorough medical history and physical examination be taken in order to properly evaluate a suspected case of gynecomastia (Table 4.3).

Table 4.3 Clinical gynecomastia evaluation (modified from Johnson and Murad, 2009)

Medical history	Localized symptoms: palpable mass, breast tenderness or enlargement, and nipple discharge
	Duration of symptoms
	History of an undescended testis, mumps, or liver or kidney disease
	Use of medications, supplements, illicit drugs, anabolic steroids
	Any distress caused by breast condition
Physical examination	Height and weight
	Signs of feminization, current Tanner stage
	Symptoms indicative of liver disease
	Breast and overlying skin
	Regional lymph nodes
	Thyroid
	Scrotum

Once an initial evaluation has been performed and physiological, self-limited causes ruled out, serum levels of hCG, LH, testosterone and estradiol should be measured. Recommended interpretations and laboratory results and etiological diagnosis of gynecomastia are shown in Figure 4.2.

Figure 4.2 Hormone levels and interpretation of results in patients with gynecomastia

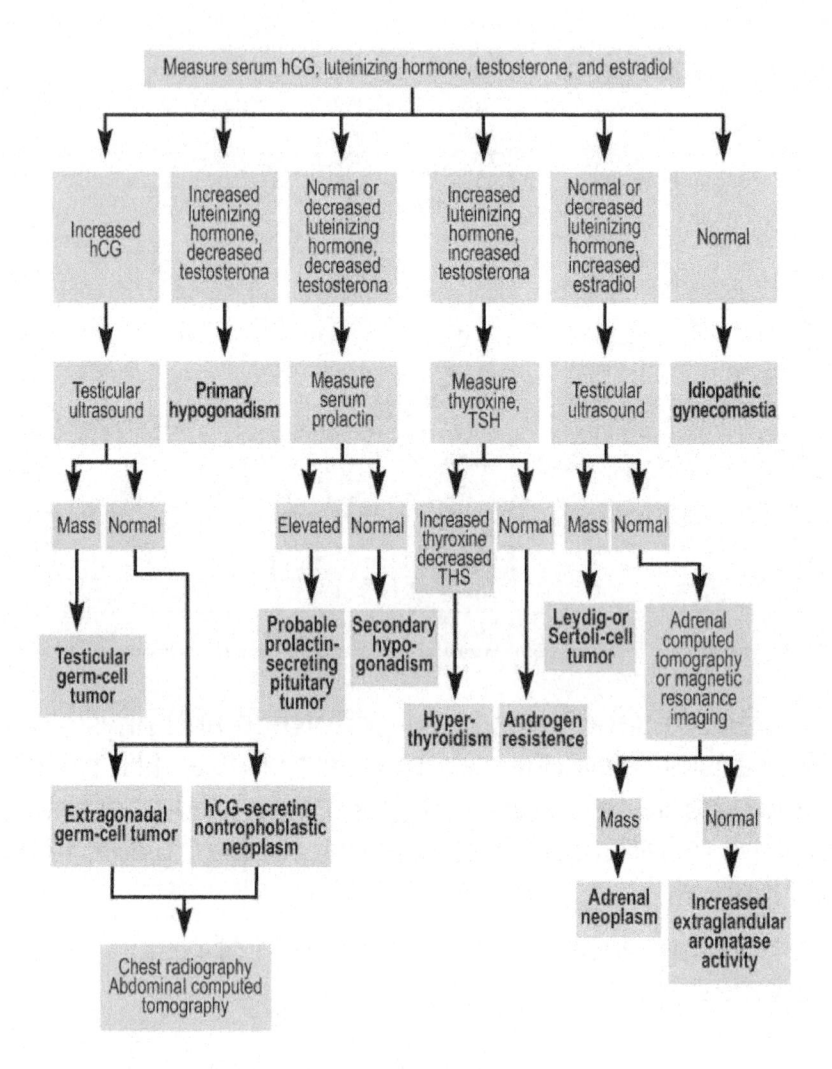

```
                    Measure serum hCG, luteinizing hormone, testosterone, and estradiol
                                              │
   ┌──────────────┬──────────────┬──────────────┬──────────────┬──────────────┐
   ▼              ▼              ▼              ▼              ▼              ▼
Increased    Increased      Normal or      Increased      Normal or       Normal
  hCG        luteinizing    decreased      luteinizing    decreased
             hormone,       luteinizing    hormone,       luteinizing
             decreased      hormone,       increased      hormone,
             testosterone   decreased      testosterone   increased
                            testosterone                  estradiol
   │              │              │              │              │              │
   ▼              ▼              ▼              ▼              ▼              ▼
Testicular    Primary       Measure       Measure       Testicular      Idiopathic
ultrasound    hypogonadism  serum         thyroxine,    ultrasound      gynecomastia
                            prolactin     TSH
   │                            │              │              │
 ┌─┴─┐                       ┌──┴──┐       ┌───┴───┐       ┌──┴──┐
 ▼   ▼                       ▼     ▼       ▼       ▼       ▼     ▼
Mass Normal              Elevated Normal Increased Normal Mass Normal
                                         thyroxine
                                         decreased
                                         THS
 │   │                       │       │     │       │       │       │
 ▼   │                       ▼       ▼     ▼       ▼       ▼       ▼
Testicular                Probable  Secondary              Leydig-or  Adrenal
germ-cell                 prolactin- hypo-                 Sertoli-cell computed
tumor                     secreting  gonadism              tumor      tomography
                          pituitary                                   or magnetic
                          tumor                                       resonance
                                             │       │                imaging
                                             ▼       ▼                   │
                                          Hyper-  Androgen             ┌─┴─┐
                                          thyroidism resistence        ▼   ▼
 │   │                                                              Mass Normal
 ▼   ▼                                                               │     │
Extragonadal hCG-secreting                                           ▼     ▼
germ-cell    nontrophoblastic                                      Adrenal Increased
tumor        neoplasm                                              neoplasm extraglandular
                                                                            aromatase
       │                                                                    activity
       ▼
Chest radiography
Abdominal computed
tomography
```

hCG: Human Chorionic Gonadotropin hormone; LH: Luteinizing Hormone; TSH: Thyroid-Stimulating Hormone.

Treatment of gynecomastia is dependent upon etiology. To treat gynecomastia for cosmetic reasons or analgesia, subcutaneous mastectomy, ultrasound-assisted liposuction, or suction-assisted lipectomy is recommended. For nonphysiological gynecomastia, discontinuation of causative medications or substances is recommended whenever possible.

Prognosis

Prognosis may depend on etiology and initiation of treatment. Physiological gynecomastia in newborns and adolescents is self-limited. For other etiologies, treatment or intervention should be initiated during the proliferative phase of breast tissue enlargement, when regression is possible. Breast size reduction can be observed in patients with medication- or substance-induced gynecomastia one month after discontinuation of the agent. If gynecomastia has been present for one year or more, substantial breast tissue regression is unlikely to occur despite pharmacotherapy (Braunstein, 2007).

Special concerns

Psychological or emotional sequelae may result from altered appearance. Because of the imbalance between estrogens and androgens, patients with gynecomastia are at greater risk of developing male breast cancer when compared with the general population.

Hirsutism-overview

Hirsutism is a common endocrine disorder characterized by excessive growth of terminal hair in a male-pattern. Terminal hair is medullated, longer, stiff, and pigmented, as opposed to vellus hair that is non medullated, short, soft, and lightly pigmented. Hirsutism results from an interaction between plasma androgen hormones and hair follicles' sensitivity to these hormones via the androgen receptor. Excess androgen causes overproduction and secretion of androgens from the adrenal glands or ovaries. Overproduction is usually triggered by altered levels of ACTH, FSH, or LH. If the disorder developed in utero, the patient may have been born with ambiguous genitalia and one of three forms of virilizing congenital adrenal hyperplasia: 21-hydroxylase deficiency, 11-hydroxylase deficiency, and 3-β hydroxysteroid and dehydrogenase deficiency.

Abnormal hormone levels leading to hirsutism are most often caused by polycystic ovarian syndrome, an idiopathic condition in which the ovaries become enlarged and the outer edges are covered with numerous cysts. Adrenal or ovarian tumors and Cushing syndrome are other etiological factors. Lastly, the use of certain substances and medications can also trigger the disorder. These include anabolic steroids, phenytoin, minoxidil, diazoxide, cyclosporine, hexachlorobenzene, and Danazol.

Epidemiology

Hirsutism prevalence is approximately 10 % in premenopausal women, although this number may vary according to race and ethnicity. Polycystic ovarian syndrome occurs in 5 % of women of reproductive age. Congenital adrenal hyperplasia occurs approximately once in every 15,000 births, and is the etiological factor behind 5 % of women diagnosed with hyperandrogenism. Androgen-secreting tumors are responsible for 0.2 % of hirsute patients.

Symptoms

The most obvious symptom underlying hirsutism is a male-pattern hair growth in women on the abdomen, face, and back. Additional symptoms depend on etiology. If hirsutism is caused by hyperandrogenism, patients may present with irregular menstrual periods, acne, deepening voice, male pattern baldness, clitoromegaly, and enlarged shoulder muscles. If the cause is Cushing's syndrome, patients may present with obesity, hypertension, DM, and thinning skin.

Guidelines on evaluation and management of hirsutism

An accurate evaluation of hirsutism and its etiology is dependent upon a careful medical history and physical examination. Age of thelarche, menarche, and menstrual history are important factors, and the onset and rate of progression of hirsutism should be determined. Androgen-mediated hirsutism is rarely associated with regular menstruation cycles (Loriaux, 2012).

According to the 2008 Endocrine Society guidelines Evaluation and Treatment of Hirsutism in Premenopausal Women, the disorder can be evaluated as mild, moderate, or severe using the Ferriman-Gallwey scoring system (Figure 4.3a). Recommendations for evaluation, diagnosis and management are shown in Figure 4.3b.

Figure 4.3a The Ferriman-Gallwey hirsutism scoring system

Separate scores of each the nine body parts need to be added to determine a hormonal hirsutism score.

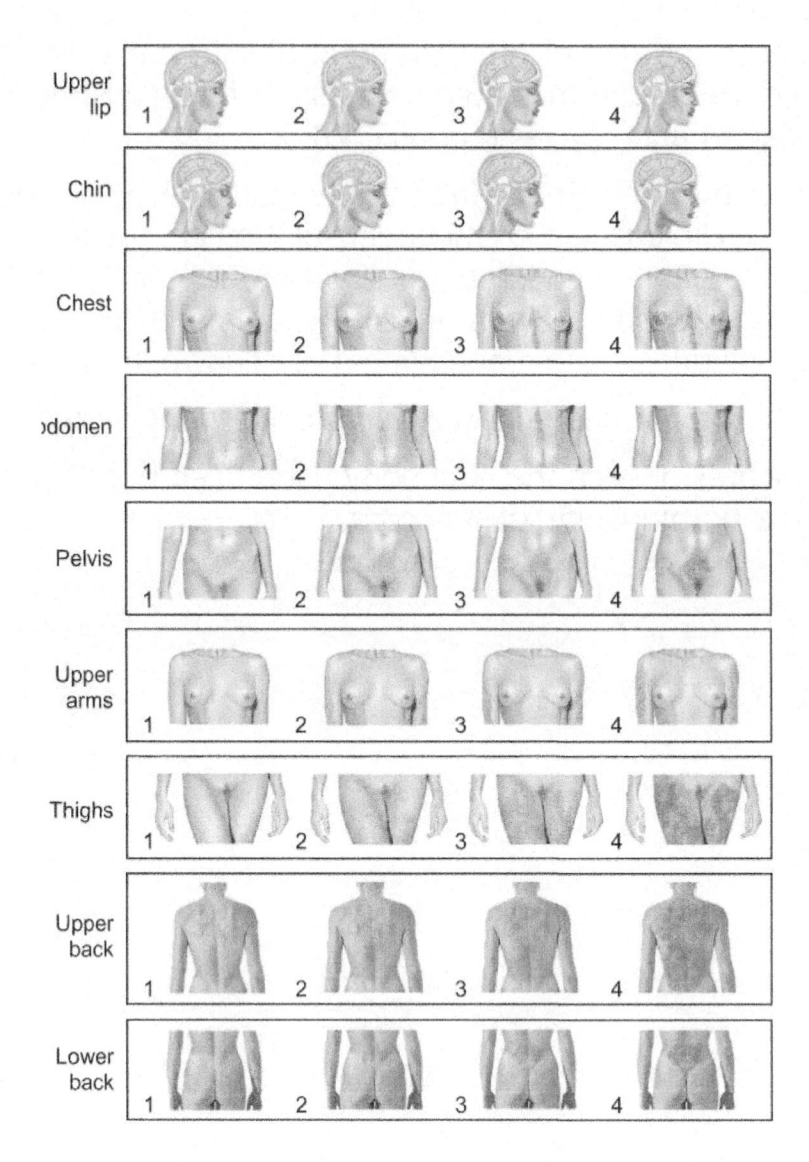

Figure 4.3b Evaluation, diagnosis and management of hirsutism (Martin et al., 2008)

```
                        Initial Evaluation of Hirsutism
    ┌──────┬──────────┬──────────┬──────────┬──────────┬──────────┐
   Drug   Hirsutism  Hirsutism  Neoplasm   Polycystic    Other
   use      mild     ≥ moderate   risk       ovary    endocrinopathy risk
         (score 8-15)(score > 15) Sudden onset, syndrome risk  History or signs
                                rapid progression, Menstrual  suggestive of
                                virilization,  irregularity or congenital adrenal
                                abdominal of pelvic infertility, hyperplasia, cortisol
                                   mass    acne, seborrhea,   excess,
                                            balding, central hyperprolactinemia
                                            obesity, acanthosis growth hormone
                                              nigricans    excess, thyroid
                                                           dysfunction
```

- Drug use → Discontinue if possible
- Testosterone blood level in early AM
  - Testosterone normal*
  - Testosterone elevated → Endocrine work-up accordingly

Trial of cosmetic, dermatologic, or oral contraceptive therapy

* If risk factors present of emerge or hirsutism worsens. Specialty laboratory total and free testosterone blood level in early AM

Course stable or improving*

Idiopathic hirsutism

Hyperandrogenemia

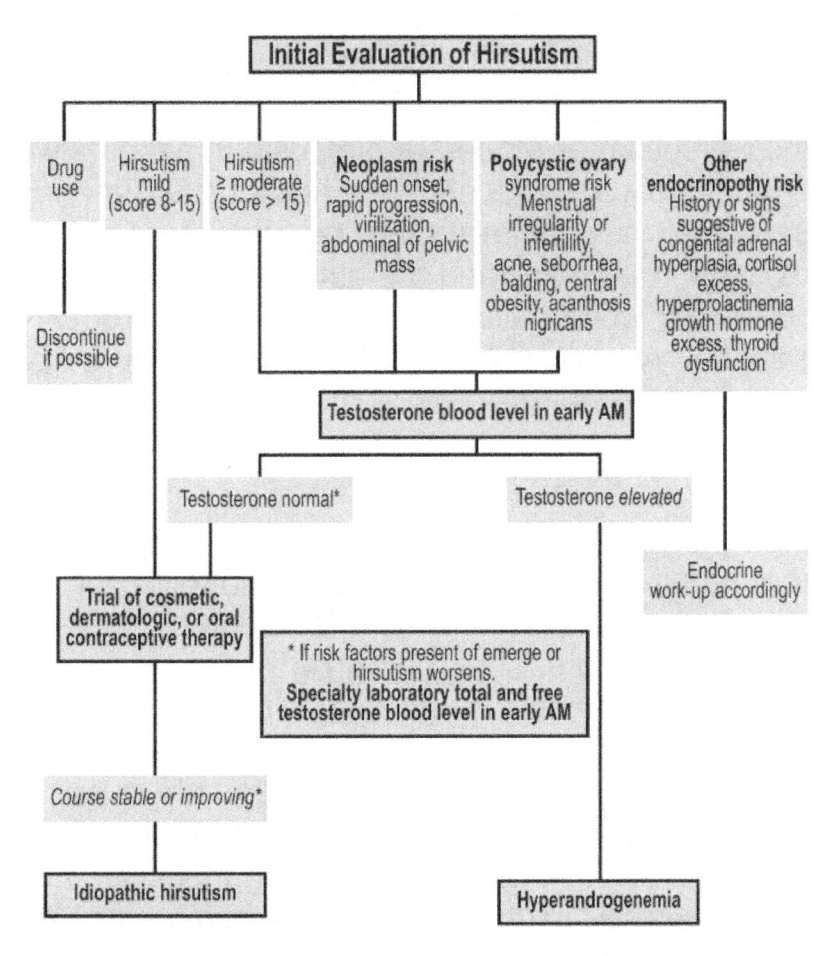

A complete evaluation of a hirsute patient should determine if testing for hyperandrogenism is needed. Women with mild hirsutism and regular menses have a very low likelihood of excess androgen levels. Patients with moderate or severe hirsutism and other symptoms indicative of an underlying disorder are more likely to be hyperandrogenic. The Endocrine Society recommends measurement of serum androgen levels for any of the following situations: moderate or severe hirsutism, rapid onset or progression, menstrual irregularity or infertility, central obesity, acanthosis nigricans, and clitoromegaly. Investigative biochemical and genetic testing will help determine the etiological factors of this and any other endocrine dysfunction.

To treat mild hirsutism or moderate hirsutism in patients with normal serum testosterone levels, the Endocrine Society recommends direct hair removal (shaving, depilatory creams, electrolysis, laser treatment) and the administration of oral contraceptives. For women diagnosed with hyperandrogenism who choose direct hair removal therapy, pharmacotherapy is also recommended to limit hair re-growth.

Prognosis

Hirsutism prognosis is dependent upon etiology. It is a chronic disorder that requires long-term treatment and follow-up. Oral contraceptive therapy can stabilize the condition by preventing new hair growth and slowing existing hair growth. Electrolysis and laser hair removal are permanent. If hirsutism is caused by adrenal or ovarian tumors, outcome will depend on prompt diagnosis, the nature of the tumor (benign or malignant), and effective surgical removal. Patients with congenital adrenal hyperplasia will most likely require lifelong cortisone treatment. Stopping medication or substance use causing hirsutism can reverse symptoms (Martin et al., 2008).

Special concerns

The Endocrine Society does not recommend the use of flutamide therapy, topical anti-androgens, or insulin-lowering drugs for treatment of hirsutism. They also recommend against the administration of GnRH agonists except in women with severe forms of hyperandrogenism.

Hirsutism may be symptomatic of underlying medical disorders (other than hyperandrogenism) that require specific treatment and might impact fertility or health status. Genetic counseling may be required (Martin et al., 2008).

Erectile dysfunction-overview

Erectile dysfunction (ED; formerly referred to as impotence) is a common health problem characterized by a man's inability to maintain an erection for sexual activity. Men with mild ED can occasionally achieve a full erection, but usually maintain an inadequate erection or no erection at all. Men with moderate ED report infrequent satisfaction with their sexual performance and that their ability to maintain an erection is moderately decreased. Men with severe ED are rarely able to achieve an erection. Etiology can be anatomical, physiological, or psychological. For instance, spinal cord or pelvic injuries, and prostate or pelvic surgery can damage nerves or arteries needed to maintain an erection. Underlying medical conditions such as hypertension, artheriosclerosis, or hypercholesterolemia can cause ED. Endocrine dysfunction and hormonal imbalance resulting in less testosterone causes ED, as well as DM, hypothyroidism, Cushing's disease, and hypogonadism. Medication or substance use also causes ED (Table 4.4). Psychological causes may include depression, performance anxiety, and situational sexual problems.

Table 4.4 Agents associated with erectile dysfunction

Medication or substance
Alcohol
Anti-anxiety medications
Anticancer medications
Cocaine
Estrogens
Ganglionic and adrenergic (beta) blockers
Monoamine oxidase inhibitors and tricyclic antidepressants
Narcotic pain relievers
Narcotics
Thiazide diuretics
Calcium channel blockers
Sedatives

Epidemiology

ED prevalence increases with age. Approximately 52 % of men aged 40–70 years suffer from ED at any given time. About 17 % experience mild ED, 25 % moderate ED, and 10 % severe ED (Araujo et al., 2000).

Symptoms

Men with ED are unable to maintain an erection needed for penetration. Some patients also report decreased libido, depression, and/or are considered obese according to the BMI index.

Guidelines on ED diagnosis and management

An official diagnosis of ED is confirmed when a patient reports that he has been unable to consistently maintain an erection for at least three-months. If surgery or injury is associated with onset, the diagnosis may be made prior to this time. The international consensus ED recommendations, Summary of the Recommendations on Sexual Dysfunction in Men, indicate that a patient's medical, sexual, and psychosocial history, as well as a complete physical examination, are all essential in diagnosing and evaluating ED. The following laboratory tests are also recommended: fasting glucose, cholesterol, lipids, and a hormone profile (Montorsi et al., 2010).

Psychotherapy, pharmacotherapy, vacuum constriction devices (VCD), and surgery may be used to treat ED. Psychotherapy should address discontinuation of pharmacotherapy (if using), reduce or eliminate performance anxiety, address situational sexual dysfunction, and implement psycho-education or modification of sexual scripts (Montorsi et al., 2010).

For pharmacotherapy, the guidelines recommend phosphodiesterase type 5 inhibitors for oral use. Alprostadil, papaverine, and a combination of phentolamine and a vasoactive intestinal polypeptide are recommended medications for intracavernosal injection therapy. ED due to endocrine dysfunction should be treated appropriately according to the underlying medical condition. The British Society for Sexual Medicine (BSSM) recommends that men with a total serum testosterone 12 nmol/l might benefit from up to a 6 months trial of testosterone replacement therapy (BSSM, 2009).

VCDs use negative pressure to fill the penis with blood and constrictive rings to trap it. The British Society for Sexual Medicine Guidelines recommend a combination of VCD and phosphodiesterase type 5 inhibitors for initial treatment of ED.

Surgical approaches to treating ED include arterial revascularization or penile prosthetic surgery. The latter is recommended if pharmacotherapy is contraindicated or has failed.

Prognosis

ED prognosis is highly dependent upon etiology. Pharmacotherapy, psychotherapy, and medical intervention are usually able to address ED in over 90 % of patients, and success rates with phosphodiesterase type 5 inhibitors and intracavernosal injection therapy are high. The success rate of testosterone therapy is not known, but studies show that its use is beneficial when treating patients with hypogonadism (Jacob, 2011).

Special concerns

Testosterone therapy is contraindicated for patients with suspected or confirmed prostate cancer. ED onset is also associated with prostate cancer treatment, and in particular radial prostatectomy. Physicians should provide a realistic time frame for recovery of ED post-surgery. Studies demonstrate that ED clinically correlates with coronary artery disease (CAD). Therefore, patients with ED should be assessed for CAD risks and be treated as needed (Montorsi et al., 2010).

Conclusion

Alterations in endocrine reproductive function are a part of the normal aging process. Menopause is part of female endocrine aging, and post menopausal status is usually attained in women over 50 years. Erectile dysfunction prevalence increases with age, affecting more than half of the male population. The common endocrine disorders hirsutism (in women) and gynecomastia (in men) are characterized by sex hormone imbalances and presentation of secondary sexual characteristics usually accorded to the opposite sex.

Chapter 5: Genetics, Epigenetics and Endocrinology

Introduction

The endocrine system can be divided into three components according to hormone action and response: synthesis and release, circulation, and target tissue levels and target organ response. Free hormone levels in target tissues or organs provide positive and negative feedback loops that determine inhibition or stimulation of hormone synthesis. Genetics were once considered the only factors influencing naturally occurring differences in hormone action and response. However, gene variability and mutations can not fully explain the wide range in responses to stimuli. It now widely accepted that genetics, epigenetics, and the environment work together in controlling the endocrine system.

Endocrine genetics

Genes expressed during endocrine gland development or genes that encode hormones, hormone receptors, and endocrine-associated factors involved in target organ response all contribute to the genetic variability that constitutes an individual's endocrine system and contributes to polymorphisms within a population.

Polymorphisms or gene mutations that are inherited are irreversible. Mutations that impair hormone synthesis and delivery can cause endocrine disorders. Genetic variability in endocrine genes is also acquired from the environment exogenously (e.g. UV rays) or endogenously via reactive oxygen species released during metabolism (Zhang and Ho, 2011).

Endocrine epigenetics

Epigenetics provides the link between inherited and acquired genetic variability by acting on the genome without altering the coding DNA sequence itself. Epigenetics refer to the hereditable mechanisms that emit changes to a gene's immediate environment, resulting in altered gene transcription. DNA methylation, histone modifications, and microRNAs (miRs) are three epigenetic chromatin-altering processes implicated in control of the endocrine system. Histone modifications carried out by histone acetyltransferases (HATs) activate gene transcription and histone deacetylases (HDACs) turn off gene transcription. Hypermethylation of CpG islands in gene promoter regions silence genes. Recent studies suggest that miR expression is also epigenetically involved in endocrine gene control. MiRs bind to target mRNA molecules and degrade their targets in order to suppress gene translation.

Epigenetics and the environment are closely associated. To maintain homeostasis, the endocrine system must readily accept cues from its surroundings. Environmental changes choreograph epigenetic regulation of genes in endocrine tissues that will in turn adapt or develop in response to the environmental stimuli (Figure 5.1).

Figure 5.1 Endocrine stimuli and responses are influenced by genetic, epigenetic and environmental factors (Zhang and Ho, 2012)

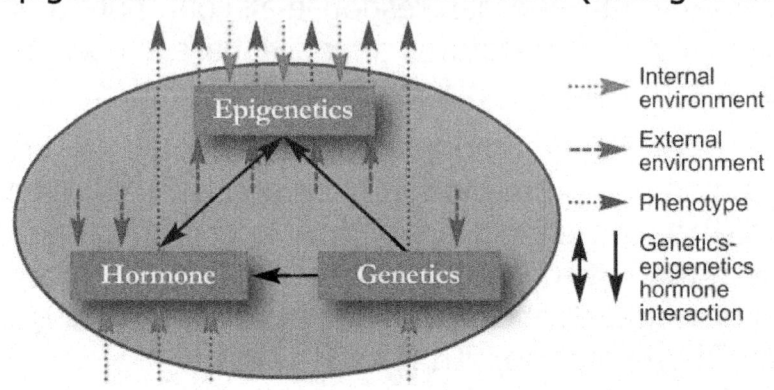

Adaptation and changes in endocrine tissues usually occur during developmental stages in utero, during puberty, or pregnancy. Because epigenetics are environmentally influenced and DNA sequences are unaltered, epigenetic control over endocrine-associated genes is versatile and reversible. This allows for flexibility in treatment and possible intervention strategies when endocrine disorders are considered (Zhang and Ho, 2011). In all, epigenetics influence the expression of genes involved in hormone biosynthesis and transport, as well as nuclear receptor expression in hormone-sensitive organs (Table 5.1). Importantly, the epigenetic regulation of some genes is heritable, affecting genes in the next generation.

Table 5.1 Endocrine genes regulated by epigenetics (modified from Zhang and Ho, 2012)

Hormone action	Enzyme	Gene	Affected cells, tissues or associated disorders
Endocrine-associated enzyme	P450scc	*CYP11A1**	*Ovarian follicles*
	3β-hydroxysteroid dehydrogenase	*HSD3B1**	*Ovarian follicles*
	17α-hydroxylase	*CYP11B2**	*Hepatoma cells, adrenal cortex*
	Aromatase	*CYP19A1**	*Ovarian follicles, endometrial and endometrionic stromal cells, breast adipose fibroblasts, hepatoma cells*
	Vitamin D synthesis	*CYP27B1**	*Human embryonic kidney derived 293F cells*
Hormone or nuclear receptors	AR	*AR**	*Prostate, endometrial*
	Estrogen receptor 1	*ESR1****	*Breast*
	Estrogen receptor 2	*ESR2**	*Prostate, breast, ovaries*
	Progesterone receptor	*PGR**	*Prostate, endometrial*
	Glucocorticoid receptor	*NR3C1****	*Brain disorder; obesity*
	Mineralocorticoid receptor	*NR3C2****	*Testes*
	Retinoic acid receptor-α	*RARA**	*Leukemia*
	Retinoic acid receptor-β	*RARB**	*Gastric and esophageal cancer*
	Retinoic acid receptor-γ**	*RARG***	*Senescence*
	Retinoid X receptor-α**	*RXRA***	*Liver fibrosis*
Peptide hormone synthesis location: Hypothalamus	Somatostatin	*SST**	*Esophageal carcinogenesis, colon cancer*
	ADH	*VAP**	*Alcohol dependence*

Hormone action	Enzyme	Gene	Affected cells, tissues or associated disorders
Pituitary	MSH	POMC*	Anorexia nervosa, ectopic ACTH syndrome, Cushing's syndrome
Gastrointestinal	Secretin	SCT*	Cell lines
	INS	INS***	Pancreatic β-cells and β-cell lines
Adipocyte	Leptin	LEP/OB*	Osteoarthritic chondrocytes, adipose, leukocytes, preadipocyte maturation
	Oxytocin receptor	OXTR*	
	FSH	FSHR*	
	IGF-1R	IGF1R***	
		IGF2R***	

ACTH: Adrenocorticotropic Hormone; ADH: Antidiuretic Hormone; AR: Androgen Receptor; FSH: Follicle-Stimulating Hormone, IGF-1R: Insulin-like Growth Factor 1 Receptor; INS: Insulin; MSH: Melanocyte-Stimulating Hormone. * regulated by methylation; ** regulated by miRNAs; *** regulated by both.

Epigenetics and endocrine disrupters

Endocrine disrupters are environmental chemicals that mimic hormone or anti-hormone activities. They contribute to epigenetic control over endocrine-associated genes. Some produce estrogenic, androgenic, anti-androgenic effects, or disrupt thyroid balance and homeostasis. Others interrupt steroid hormone metabolism. Sources include manmade substances, plants and plant-derived molecules, food, water, and air. It is postulated that endocrine disrupters detrimentally influence growth, development, metabolism, and reproduction. Table 5.2 lists known endocrine disrupters and their effects on the endocrine system.

Table 5.2 Endocrine disrupters (Zhang and Ho, 2012)

Disrupter	Routes of exposure	Hormonal effect
Phytoestrogens	Soybean	Estrogenic, anti-estrogenic
Diethystilbestrol (DES)	Drug	Estrogenic
Bisphenol A (BPA)	Food/plastic	Estrogenic
Polybrominated diphenyl ethers (PBDEs)	House dust/flame retardants	Estrogen, thyroid hormone imbalance
Dioxins	Food, air, water/combustion	Estrogenic, anti-estrogenic
Polychlorinated biphenyls (PCBs)	Food/coolants and lubricants	Estrogenic, anti-estrogenic, thyroid hormone homeostasis
Perfluorooctanoic acid (PFOA)	Surfactant	Estrogenic
Heavy metals	Industry, cigarettes, food, soil	Estrogenic
Polycyclic aromatic hydrocarbons (PAHs)	Air, food	Steroid metabolism
Dichlorodiphenyl-trichloroethane (DTT)	Food/pesticide	Anti-androgenic
Vinclozolin	Fungicide	Anti-androgenic

The genetics and epigenetics of growth and metabolism

The genetics of growth

Human GH is encoded by two genes: GH1 and GH2. GH1 encodes mature GH, the major form of GH expressed in the pituitary gland. Alternatively spliced GH1 products are also expressed in the pituitary gland but are considered minor forms. GH2 differs slightly from GH1 and is only expressed in the placenta. It replaces the circulating GH1 gene product at mid-pregnancy. Both gene products stimulate cell growth and proliferation, and are of particular importance in utero and during childhood. GHR, GHRH, GHRHR, IGF-1, IGF-2, IGF-1R, and IGF-2R gene products promote growth and proliferation in almost all cell types (Mullis, 2011).

GH or IGF deficiencies

Alterations in any of the aforementioned genes that result in low levels of GH or IGF-1 can cause growth disorders and diminished stature. At least 34 deletions and single-base pair substitutions are known in GH1 alone. In addition, mutations in the GH secretagogue receptor (GHSR), the homeobox gene (HESX1), Sox3 (SOX3) and the muscarinic acetylcholine receptor (mAchR) are associated with low levels of GH or IGF-1, and impaired growth in children (Mullis, 2011).

The epigenetics of growth

Little is known about the epigenetic regulation of GH and GH-associated genes. However, several studies report that the IGF1R and IGF2R are subjected to two forms of epigenetic control. The genes promoters' are hypermethylated in prostate cancer cells, and the transcripts are targeted by degradative miRs (Zhang and Ho, 2012).

The genetics of thyroid function

Mutations in genes responsible for thyroid hormone synthesis, secretion and response can all cause thyroid dysfunction. Known mutations causing impaired thyroid hormone action and response, as well as hyperthyroidism and hypothyroidism are listed in Table 5.3.

Table 5.3 Genes associated with hyperthyroidism and hypothyroidism

Phenotype	Gene	Mechanism	Associated disorders
Thyroid hormone synthesis	TTF1, PAX8, TTF2/FOXE1	Thyroid-specific gene regulation	
	TPO	Iodide organification	
	TG	Structural prohormone	
	NIS	Iodide transport from blood to thyroid cells	
	PDS	Iodide transport from blood to follicular lumen	Sensorial deafness (Pendred syndrome)
	DUOX1/THOX1, DUOX2/THOX2	Thyroidal hydrogen peroxide generation	
	DEHAL1	Deiodination for iodide recycling	
Impaired hypothalamic-pituitary-thyroid axis	LHX3	Early pituitary development	CPHD, pituitary mass, rigid cervical spine
	LHX4		CPHD, sella turcica defect
	PROP1	Pituitary cell lineage expression	CPHD, pituitary mass
	POU1F	Generation and cell-type specification	GH, PRL deficiency
	HESX1, PHF6	Forebrain, midline and pituitary development	Septo-optic dysplasia, chronic pulmonary heart disease, epilepsy
	TRHR	Thyrotropin-releasing hormone receptor	
	TSHB	Thyrotropin β subunit	
Transient congenital hypothyroidism	DUOX2/THOX2	Partially defective hydrogen peroxide production	-
Permanent hyperthyroidism	TSHR	Thyrotropin receptor gain-of-function mutation	GHD
Predisposition or association to/with hyperthyroidism	HLA region	Major histocompatibility region, HLA class I and class II molecules	GHD
	PTPN22	Protein tyrosine phosphatase, non-receptor type 22	

Phenotype	Gene	Mechanism	Associated disorders
	CTLA4	cytotoxic T-lymphocyte-associated protein 4	
	CD40	CD40 molecule, TNF receptor superfamily member 5	
	TSHR	Thyrotropin receptor gain-of-function mutation	
	TG	Structural prohormone	
	FCRL3	FC receptor-like-3 protein	
	SCGB3A2	Secretory uteroglobin-related protein 1	

CPHD: Combined Pituitary Hormone Deficiency; GH: Growth Hormone; GHD: Growth Hormone Disorder; PRL: Prolactin.

The epigenetics of thyroid function

The epigenetic regulation of thyroid-specific genes contributes to tumor suppression, iodide transport, and iodine metabolism. Dysregulation can lead to thyroid cancer. For example, the TSHR promoter is hypermethylated and silenced in thyroid carcinomas, and iodide transporter genes SLC5A5 and SLC26A4 are methylated and down-regulated in thyroid tumors. In addition, CpG islands in the cell cycle regulating CDKN4 and RASSF1A gene promoters are methylated in 30 % of thyroid neoplasms, and the fibroblast growth factor receptor 2 gene (FGFR2) is also silenced by methylation. Lastly, epigenetics coordinate activation of tumor-promoting genes in the thyroid. For instance, histone H3 methylation and deacetylation negatively regulate MAGE-A3/6 promoters in thyroid carcinomas (Kondo et al., 2008).

The genetics and epigenetics of the parathyroid function

Genetic and epigenetic dysfunction in parathyroid hormone synthesis, secretion, and response affect calcium and phosphate metabolism. They can also lead to hyperparathyroidism and hypoparathyroidism.

Heterozygous mutations in CASR cause familial hypocalciuric hypercalcemia (FHH) and homozygous mutations cause neonatal severe hyperparathyroidism (NSHPT). In addition, mutations or altered expression of the MEN1, PTEN, RB, HRAS, p53, and CCDN1 genes can cause formation of benign parathyroid adenomas that lead to primary hyperparathyroidism. Lastly, parathyroid carcinomas causing hyperparathyroidism are often traced to mutations in HRPT2, or hypermethylation of the APC tumor suppressor gene (Westin et al., 2009).

Isolated hypoparathyroidism can be genetically explained by PTH, GCMB, or SOX3 mutations, as well as gain-of-function mutations in CASR. Importantly, hypoparathyroidism is a symptom displayed in patients with DiGeorge syndrome (in which the 22q11.2 region encoding the TBX1 gene on chromosome 22 is deleted), Sanjad–Sakati syndrome (mutations in the TCBE or GATA3 genes), and polyglandular autoimmune syndrome (mutations in AIRE) (De Sanctis et al., 2012).

The epigenetics of pseudohypoparathyroidism

Several studies report that a certain form of pseudohypoparathyroidism is caused in part by the epigenetic regulation of the GNAS gene. Patients with this disorder show differentially methylated regions at this locus (Izzi et al., 2012).

The genetics and epigenetics of pancreatic function

Genes encoding INS and glucagon are differentially regulated and expressed according to pancreatic cell type: α cells secrete glucagon, and β cells secrete INS. All three major types of epigenetic gene regulation are observed in pancreatic cells; DNA methylation, histone-modifying enzymes, and miRs regulate pancreatic development, β cell function, and β cell proliferation (Gilbert and Liu, 2012; Guay et al., 2012).

As pancreatic dysfunction can lead to T1D and T2D, countless studies have focused on the genetic and epigenetic causes of DM subtypes. Because of its association with T2D, obesity is often co-examined.

The genetics of T2D and obesity

Obesity and DM are genetically intertwined and both are partially hereditable. Parental T2D and obesity can increase the risk in offspring three- and two-fold, respectively (Drong et al., 2012). Evidence relating the two disorders to lifestyle and environmental factors is also clear, suggesting that epigenetic regulation is equally important.

Over 150 genetic loci are associated with T2D and obesity, and related traits include fasting glucose, insulin secretion, BMI, and birth weight. Early successes in identifying causative genes have come from studying extreme monogenic or syndromic forms of both disorders. It is now accepted that maturity-onset diabetes results from mutations in two genes: HNF1A (hepatocyte nuclear factor-1A) and GCK (glucokinase). Combined genome wide association studies (GWAS) have identified other gene variants considered risk loci. For example, the TCF7L2 (transcription factor 7-like 2) gene is associated with a two-fold increase in T2D risk between homozygote groups.

Identifying specific genes in varying, milder forms of either disorder by large-scale association has proved difficult. Some 40 genes cause T1D, and an equal number have been identified for T2D. Some of the known genes that cause different diabetes subtypes are listed in Table 5.4.

Diabetes subtype	Complex/Enzyme/RNA	Causal genes
T1D	Major histocompatibility complex INS Protein tyrosine phosphatase, non-receptor type 22	HLA region genes INS PPTN22 Others
T2D	Transcription factor 7-like 2 CDK5 regulatory subunit associated protein 1-like 1 cyclin-dependent kinase inhibitor 2A cyclin-dependent kinase inhibitor 2B Melatonin receptor 1B Potassium inwardly-rectifying channel, subfamily J, member 11	TCF7L2 CDKAL1 CDKN2A CDKN2B MTNR1B KCNJ11 Others
Latent autoimmune diabetes in adults	Major histocompatibility complex INS Protein tyrosine phosphatase, non-receptor type 22	HLA region genes INS PPTN22

INS: Insulin; T1D: Type 1 Diabetes; T2D: Type 2 Diabetes.

Only a small number of variable loci that specifically cause obesity or are associated with BMI have been identified. The FTO (fat mass and obesity-associated) locus has been associated with a 2.5 kg weight difference between homozygote groups (McCarthy, 2010). However, several studies suggest that a nearby gene RPGRIP1L may be partially responsible. Both genes are expressed in the hypothalamus, and RPGRIP1L responds to changes in nutrition and hormone levels (McCarthy, 2010).

The epigenetics of T2D and obesity

Several genes related to T2D and obesity are epigenetically controlled by DNA methylation. This heritable form of gene regulation can increase the risk of either DM or obesity in future generations if a mother is diabetic while pregnant. T2D- and obesity-associated candidate genes regulated by DNA methylation are listed in Table 5.5. In summary, many loci are differentially methylated in diseased pancreatic islets from T2D patients (Volkmar et al, 2012), whereas differential methylation in obesity is observed in several blood cell types (summarized in Drong et al., 2012).

Table 5.5 Type 2 diabetes- and obesity-associated genes epigenetically regulated by DNA methylation (modified from Drong et al., 2012)

Disorder	Genes	Phenotypes
DM	CCL2	T2D
	INS	T2D
	PDX1	T2D
	PPARGC1A	T2D
Obesity	ALOX12, ALPL, BCL2A1, CASP10, CAV1, CCL3, CD9, CDKN1C, DSC2, EPHA1, EVI2A, HLA, IRF5, KRT1, LCN2, MLLT4, MMP9, MPL, NID1, NKX31, PMP22, S100A12, TAL1, VIM	BMI, fat mass, and lean mass
	KCNQ1OT1, H19, IGF2, GRB10, MEST, SNRPN, GNAS, MCHR1	BMI
	POMC	Obesity
	IL8, NOS3, PIK3CD, RXRA, SOD1	Fat mass and % fat mass
	SLC6A4	BMI, weight, waist circumference
	TACSTD2	Fat mass

BMI: Body Mass Index; T2D: Type 2 Diabetes.

Many epigenome-wide association studies are underway to identify more loci that are epigenetically controlled in people who have T2D or who are obese. Data show that hypermethylated loci are also implicated in the genetics of the both disorders. Studies with larger sample sizes and relevant tissue or cell type samples will confirm ties between genetic, environmental, and epigenetic factors.

The genetics and epigenetics of reproductive endocrinology

Genetics, epigenetics, and environmental factors all influence sexual reproduction, sexual development, and sexual characteristics. They also impact the natural aging of the reproductive systems in both men and women, or disorders that arise from any impaired sexual reproduction and function.

The genetics and epigenetics of menopause

Menopause is the final stage of reproductive aging in women. Its onset in women usually aged 40 years or above is variable but highly heritable. GWAS have discovered at least 30 new loci and related traits implicated in the natural onset of menopause, early menopause, and primary ovarian insufficiency. Table 5.6 lists 17 loci associated with menopausal onset identified in a meta-analysis of 22 GWAS (Stolk et al., 2012; Perry et al., 2013). The known gene products function in DNA repair or immune function. Others may be involved in ovarian aging.

Table 5.6 Genes associated with the natural onset of menopause

Pathway/Function	Enzyme	Gene
Cell proliferation	-	rs7333181 on chromosome 13
Possibly contribute ovarian aging	BR serine/threonine kinase 1	BRSK1
	Transmembrane protein 150B	TMEM224
	Suppressor of variegation 4-20 homolog 2	SUV420H2
DNA Repair	Exonuclease 1	EXO1
	Helicase, POLQ-like	HELQ
	ubiquitin interaction motif containing 1	UIMC1
	family with sequence similarity 175, member	FAM175A
	tousled-like kinase 1	TLK1
	Fanconi anemia group I protein	FANCI
	DNA polymerase subunit gamma-1	POLG
	Primase, DNA, polypeptide 1	PRIM1

Pathway/Function	Enzyme	Gene
Immune function	Interleukin 11	IL11
	NLR family, pyrin domain containing 11	NLRP11
	Proline-rich coiled-coil 2A	BAT2
Unknown	Minichromosome maintenance complex component 8	MCM8
	-	5q35.2

Several candidate gene studies on menopause have focused on estrogen biosynthesis and vascular pathways, but have yielded conflicting results. Evidence implicating polymorphisms of the CYP1B1 and CYP19A1genes (encoding members of the cytochrome P450 family) with age at natural menopause onset is more concrete (He and Murabito, 2012).

Epigenetics, epigenetic disrupters, and menopause

Some epigenetic disruptors mimicking epigenetic regulation of endocrine genes have estrogenic and anti-estrogenic properties. Estrogenicity or androgenicity is the ability of a compound to bind to the estrogen or androgen receptors and initiate or inhibit transcription (McLachlan et al., 2006). Animal studies in the laboratory and in wildlife vertebrates demonstrate that estrogenic and industrial contaminants (pesticides, plasticizers and natural phytoestrogens in plants) impact the reproductive health of both male and female reproduction systems. In females, estrogen levels are pivotal in the initiation of puberty and the onset of menopause. Recent studies have investigated the epigenetic mechanisms carried out by chemical disruptors on estrogen pathways in humans. The studies hypothesize that chemicals that mimic or block estrogen may advance puberty and breast development, as well as delay the onset of menopause (McLachlan et al., 2006).

The genetics and epigenetics of postmenopausal status

The bioavailability of endogenous estrogen drops off dramatically in postmenopausal women and corresponding changes in gene expression of several endocrine-associated enzymes have been documented. Recent GWAS link FTO and LEPR polymorphisms to weight circumference, adiposity, and SHBG (sex hormone-binding globulin) and CYP19A1 loci to postmenopausal status (Lim et al., 2012; Prescott et al., 2012). Gene expression in postmenopausal women is also linked to overall health and lifestyle factors such as diet and exercise. This suggests that epigenetic regulation plays an important role. For example, gene expression of steroid-hormone metabolism and insulin growth factor-like signaling is altered in adipose tissue from postmenopausal women that are overweight or obese (Campbell et al., 2013).

Epigenetic regulation of estrogenic pathways has also been linked to osteoporosis, breast cancer, and endometrial cancer in postmenopausal women. Clear conclusions have yet to be made in determining genetic susceptibility or environmentally influenced epigenetic regulation of associated pathways. However, risk factors and treatment of these disorders in conjunction with hormone replacement therapy in postmenopausal women remains an area of intense research.

The genetics and epigenetics of gynecomastia

Gynecomastia can arise from genetic mutations or epigenetic regulation of several endocrine-associated genes, sometimes caused by hypogonadism. Known genetic mutations that cause hypogonadism include 5α-reductase deficiency (mutations in SRD5A2), androgen insensitivity syndrome (AR mutations), hemochromatosis (HFE mutations) and Klinefelter syndrome (males with a XXY karyotype). Kallmann syndrome, a form of secondary hypogonadism, is also associated with gynecomastia. Mutations in many genes result in mild or severe forms of the disorder: KAL1, FGFR1, FGF8, PROKR2, GnRH1, TAC3, TACR3, LEP, NELF, CHD7, DAX1 and KISS-1 (Topaloglu and Kotan, 2010). Overexpression of the aromatase enzyme (encoded by CYP19A1) has also been associated with gynecomastia in boys (McLachlan et al., 2006).

The genetics and epigenetics of erectile dysfunction

Substantial evidence identifying genetic polymorphisms in patients with erectile dysfunction (ED) is lacking, and GWAS investigating ED have not yet been performed. However, ED is a vascular disorder that is often associated with cardiovascular disease (CVD), CAD, and hypertension, as well as DM, hypogonadism, hypothyroidism and hyperthyroidism. Therefore, genes associated with these conditions are sometimes linked to ED. For instance, genetic and biochemical markers of endothelial function, thrombosis, and dyslipidemia in patients with CVD are now accepted risk factors profiled in patients with ED. These included nitric oxide, asymmetric dimethylarginine, and endothelin. More specifically, the following genes are now considered candidate genetic markers for ED: angiotensin converting enzyme (ACE), endothelial nitric oxide synthase (eNOS), hSMR3A (submaxillary gland androgen regulated protein 3A), MTHFR (methylene tetrahydrofolate reductase, NADPH and GNB3 (G-protein beta-3 subunit) (Lippi et al., 2012).

There are no known studies on the epigenetic control of ED-associated genes. However, information gained with intensely studied hereditary diseases such as CVD, DM, and hypertension will most likely elucidate any epigenetic control that may exist over genes associated with the disorder.

The genetics and epigenetics of hirsutism

Genetic variability and epigenetic regulation of specific genes controlling secondary sex characteristics may cause hirsutism. These involve genes that control androgen hormone action and response. For one, polycystic ovary syndrome results from excessive amounts of androgenic hormones that may result from polymorphisms in AR. Second, congenital adrenal hyperplasia results from a 21-hydroxylase deficiency. The 21-hydroxylase enzyme is part of the P450 cytochrome c family, and polymorphisms in CYP21A2 and CYP21A1P (as well as recombinant forms) have been found in hirsute patients (Lai et al., 2012).

Hirsutism is also associated with INS resistance, T2D, and obesity. At high enough levels, INS may stimulate the production of androgen hormones in the ovaries (Lai et al., 2012). Theoretically, genetic and epigenetic evidence concerning these disorders might also be applied to hirsutism, as it is usually symptomatic of another underlying medical condition.

Conclusion

Genetics, epigenetics, and the environment contribute to endocrine system development, function, and dysfunction. Cooperation between these factors ultimately contributes to the variability seen in the endocrine system of an individual or within a population. Genetics and epigenetics underlie most endocrine disorders. Although an individual's genetic makeup is permanent, epigenetic and environmental influences are more flexible. This will allow for the possibility of more therapeutical options and medical interventions as novel determinants of endocrine dysfunction are identified.

Chapter 6: Links

Acromegaly.org www.acromegaly.org

American Diabetes Association www.diabetes.org

American Association of Clinical Endocrinologists www.aace.com

American Thyroid Association www.thyroid.org

American Urological Association www.auanet.org

Asia and Oceania Thyroid Association aothyroid.org

Association of Reproductive Health Professionals www.arhp.org

British Menopause Society www.thebms.org.uk

British Society for Sexual Medicine www.bssm.org.uk

Diabetes UK www.diabetes.org.uk

European Foundation for the Study of Diabetes www.europeandiabetesfoundation.org

European Menopause and Andropause Society www.emas-online.org

European Thyroid Association www.eurothyroid.com

European Society for Sexual Medicine www.essm.org

European Society of Endocrinology www.ese-hormones.org

Hormone Health Network www.hormone.org

International Association for the Study of Obesity www.iaso.org

International Communication Office of Pediatric Endocrine Societies www.copesinternational.org

International Diabetes Federation www.idf.org

International Federation of Gynecology & Obstetrics www.figo.org

International Menopause Society www.imsociety.org

International Obesity Task Force www.iaso.org/iotf

International Osteoporosis Foundation www.iofbonehealth.org

International Premature Ovarian Failure Association www.ipofa.org

International Society for Sexual Medicine www.issm.info

International Society of Endocrinology www.endosociety.com

Latin American Thyroid Society www.lats.org

National Parathyroid Education Foundation www.parathyroidfoundation.org

NIH Office of Rare Diseases Research www.rarediseases.info.nih.gov

North American Menopause Society www.menopause.org

Pediatric Endocrine Society www.lwpes.org

Pituitary Network Association www.pituitary.org

The Endocrine Society www.endo-society.org

The Global Genes Project globalgenes.org

The Growth Hormone Research Society www.ghresearchsociety.org

The Human Growth Foundation www.hgfound.org

Thyroid Federation International www.thyroid-fed.org

Thyroid Foundation of Canada www.thyroid.ca

World Health Organization www.who.int

WorldWIDE Diabetes www.worldwidediabetes.org

Printed in Great Britain
by Amazon